MAIN ISSUES

Confronting Christendom

MAIN ISSUES
Confronting Christendom

BY

HAROLD A. BOSLEY, Ph.D.

NEW YORK   LONDON

HARPER & BROTHERS PUBLISHERS

MAIN ISSUES CONFRONTING CHRISTENDOM

To the Congregation of

The Mount Vernon Place Methodist Church
Baltimore, Maryland

in Whose Good Fellowship

I Have Found Freedom, Inspiration, and Peace

✥ Contents ❧

✥ *Preface* ✥

There is no time now for the Christian church or any other responsible institution to emulate one of F. Scott Fitzgerald's agents who "hesitated before the wide horizon of how she might have lived." The problems at hand are so urgent and the issues involved so ominous that backward glances and nostalgic longings must be kept at a minimum in the interests of effective living today. It is probably fair, however, to sum up the tragedy of the recent past in world affairs with the simple statement: it need not have been. There was nothing inevitable about its coming. No demon thrust it upon us with irresistible and inescapable might. Orestes and Antigone—even Job—might complain about the way fate or God was dominating their lives, filling them with tragedy, but we cannot. We suffer the consequences of choices which our fathers before us and we ourselves have made, choices which have been infected with ignorance, pride, greed, and prejudice. Our sins have found us out—and not ours only but our fathers' also. Only one who disbelieves in the reality of moral order in the universe can complain that we are the victims of a cosmic injustice. This the Christian does not do. The Christian church cannot be content to seek out the wailing wall of what "might have been" and expend vital energies in either orgies of grief or emotional flights from social realities. Much less can it (like so many of our contemporaries) be hypnotized by the horror of the approaching doom of man and all his works. Even if it could be demonstrated that literally no hope for the survival of civilization remains, the Christian church would say with the Master, "We must work the work of Him who sent me, while it is day; night comes, when no one can work."

ix

That is why the church, in all its branches, is saying, "All we like sheep have gone astray. . . ." "There is none righteous, no not one. . . ." and is hard at the task of recapturing and redefining itself in terms of its historic mission, namely, the redemption of the world.

To say that this means a redesigning of pat ecclesiastical plans is to put it mildly. But we either do that in a desperate attempt to save ourselves and our civilization, or we accept disaster with docility. No one knows whether even our most strenuous efforts to redirect civilization can be successful; certainly no one in his right mind would attempt to guarantee it—even in words. But the possibility remains, and reasonable men of great faith can and will ask no more than the opportunity to work for its realization. And they will work with courage and hope, knowing that "The hidden issues of the future are with the Eternal, our God, but the unfolded issues of the day are with us and with our children." Clearly, the price of survival is a new world. It is that or no world.

This book is an attempt to clarify some of the main issues before the Christian church today. Much of the material was presented in lecture form to the Pastors' Conference held at Florida Southern College, Lakeland, Florida, in April, 1946. The ministers who attended that conference must assume some responsibility for this book since their encouragement was instrumental in its being prepared for publication.

Perhaps a word about the structure of the book is in order. Each chapter both gives a statement of some facet of the central spiritual problem of our time and suggests an answer. In each case, the responsibility of the church to lead toward a better world is stressed. This is not to say that the church can or should try to do it all alone, but it must and can take the lead in all these matters. For this cause it was brought into being and only by losing itself in this cause can the church find the kind and quality of life which it deeply desires for itself and mankind.

It is a pleasure to acknowledge the hospitality of President Ludd Spivey and Professor Charles Kraft of Florida Southern

College. I want to reserve a special word of gratitude to my teacher and long-time friend, the late Shirley Jackson Case, dean of the School of Religion at that institution, when the lectures were delivered.

The preparation of a manuscript amid the responsibilities of a pastorate would be impossible were it not for the help of the entire church staff: the secretary, Miss Ruth V. Graf, and my fellow ministers, Mr. J. Edward Moyer, Dr. William H. Litsinger, and Dr. Eugene S. Ashton. I am dedicating this book to the Mount Vernon Place Methodist Church for the good and sufficient reason that it is a living example of Paul's words, ". . . One thing I do, forgetting what lies behind and straining forward to what lies ahead, I press on toward the goal for the prize of the upward call of God in Christ Jesus."

HAROLD A. BOSLEY

Divinity School
Duke University
Durham, North Carolina

❧ *Acknowledgments* ❧

The author wishes to express his appreciation to the following authors, publishers and agents for permission to quote from their copyrighted works:

Brandt & Brandt for "Song for Three Soldiers" by Stephen Vincent Benét.

Harper & Brothers and Brandt & Brandt for the lines from *Conversation at Midnight* by Edna St. Vincent Millay.

Opinion for the lines by Paul Efrick Eldridge.

Lois Kingsley Pelton and the New York *Times* for "Iconoclast."

Religion in Life for much of the material in Chapter III.

❧§❧

MAIN ISSUES
Confronting Christendom

Chapter 1   ᡧᡦᡝᢦ   CONFRONTING THE SPIRITUAL TRAGEDY OF OUR TIME

I

Would anyone undertake to measure the heartache in the world today? And, if he could, who thinks he is strong enough to bear the knowledge? It is enough—it is too much—to know that never before have men suffered so much from every conceivable ailment of body, mind, and spirit as now. If ever there was a time when the Spirit of God was needed to fly abroad "with healing in his wings" now is that time. If Jesus has been truly designated as "the King of all the bruised hearts of men," his is a kingdom beyond the reach of measurement.

Confronted by this fact many Christians turn away in sheer fright from the challenge it brings to their faith. Yet, as we are tempted to turn away, we need to remind ourselves of Lincoln Steffens' story of the child who, when awakened out of a deep sleep, cried, "Oh dear, I have lost my place in my dreams!" We have been content too generally to dream about the Kingdom of God, to let our fancy play idly with one utopian suggestion after another while in our very midst the cry of the needy and the suffering arises unheeded if not unheard, while the poor are sold for a pair of shoes, while justice and brotherhood wander voiceless in our city. It is high time we lost our place in the sort of dreams that have kept and continue to keep us from working at the healing mission of the Christian church in an alert, realistic manner.

The Christian church can and must modestly affirm its relationship to the Great Physician. We cannot claim to know all that

I

needs to be known about the ailments of our day, but we do know that they are threatening our very life. We do not know all we should like to know about specific remedies, but we do know certain immediate and ultimately curative steps that can and should be taken. We may not be able to get the patient to co-operate, but we are under obligation to do everything in our power toward this end. We need always to remember that we do not, cannot *heal*—God alone can do that. The most that we can do it to state the steps by which His healing love can restore us to health. And to this task we now turn our attention.

II

The tragedy of the modern world is too confused, too vast, and too terrible to be compressed into any concise definition. But that fact does not relieve us of the obligation to seek a clearer understanding of it. Much less does it bring to naught our Christian conviction that this and every other age must be confronted with the redeeming will of God as we see it, both in the life and teachings of Jesus Christ and in the Christian tradition. Therefore, both because we cannot escape coming to some kind of terms with the tragedy of the modern world and because we must grapple with it "in His name and for His sake," it is the part of wisdom to seek a clearer understanding, first of its general nature, then of certain concrete forms in which we encounter it from day to day, and finally of our Christian task in the face of it all.

Two men far removed from each other in time and space, but not in spirit, Aristotle and Maxwell Anderson, can help us understand the general nature of the tragedy which has overtaken us. Aristotle made a careful study of the tragic dramas—one of the glories of ancient Greece—from the point of view of their effect upon audiences. He concluded that there are four kinds of tragedy: tragedy of plot, of suffering, of character, and of spectacle. The differences between these audience reactions grow out of real differences in the tragic events in the dramas themselves. In some dramas plot stands out as the dominant fact; in others, suffering; in others, characters; and in others, the spectacular flourish and manner of presentation.

I do not see how we can survey the drama of modern life and escape the conclusion that it is one terrible and seemingly endless tragedy of sheer suffering. But tragic suffering is much more than simple pain, as Maxwell Anderson points out. A tragic hero "must pass through an experience that opens his eyes to an error of his own. He must learn through suffering. In a tragedy he suffers death itself as a consequence of his fault and the recognition of his fault and the consequent alteration of his course of action." [1]

This is more than an apt characterization of a tragic hero like Hamlet, though it is that; it is as trenchant a description of a tragic age as we shall ever find. Was it not Livy, the Roman historian, who set his pen to the grim task of tracing the development of Roman character from its earliest period ". . . until these last days when we can endure neither our vices nor their remedies"? Did not Jesus weep over Jerusalem, the city that he sought to save, only to be balked by that stormy self-righteousness which finally proved to be its undoing? Was not Jeremiah contemplating a tragic age when he felt that the confusion around him was so great it could come from nothing less than inconsistency in God Himself: "Ah, Lord God, surely Thou hast greatly deceived this people and Jerusalem saying, Ye shall have peace, whereas the sword reacheth unto the soul"?

Not many, I think, will dissent from the conclusion that we are living in an age akin to these earlier ones; that ours, like theirs, is an age of tragic suffering; that in it "the sword" of events "reacheth unto the soul"—that basic pattern of personal and social life as envisioned by the Christian faith and implanted as ideals in Christian institutions.

And we encounter this tragedy of which the sword is an all too fit symbol in terribly concrete ways these days. Destruction, artificial idealism, despair, degeneracy, spiritual exhaustion—these suggest some of the kinds of suffering preying upon our world today.

The simple fact of *destruction* is one of the most obvious characteristics of our day. Destruction of life, ideals, homes, cities, cathedrals, libraries, museums, ships, canals, and industries. The cost of this leveling of life in a spasm of animal fury cannot be computed. We do not even attempt it. We simply behold it in the silent agony of despair. So much might have been done for the enrichment and ennoblement of human life had we been able to harness to creative efforts all the energy that has gone into these acts of destruction.

Men were nerved to face and endure the wholesale destruction of the war by forced feedings of *artificial idealism*. The great and essentially good ideals of freedom, democracy, security, the historic destiny of nations, the will of God, etc. were placed on modern prayer wheels and whirled until they lost rational content. Consider a few of the monstrous perversions of plain historical fact which sought to make the curse of total war endurable. Some are found in *Mein Kampf*; some in the speeches of Mussolini; some in the journals of Christian theology. The men who were about to die were variously told that "War is a sacrament—the divinely ordained moment when life achieves true glory"; that "War ennobles character"; that "This is a just war"; that "The Christian can only say 'Yes' to this war." A dread day of judgment is now dawning for all such war-born counsels. The outraged conscience of ethical religion is demanding a hearing, and it will make short shrift of such idealistic dodges and maneuvers as these. If we may believe recent history, cynicism rather than a new faith will take possession of many a life that depended upon these artificial ideals for its vitality.

Out of destruction and artificial idealism grows *despair*. The kind of despair that shatters the integrity of persons and peoples. The kind we see in the opening chapters of *Out of the Night*, or find a vivid chronicle of in a book which we ought to be rereading these days: *All Quiet on the Western Front*. In one poignant section the young German soldier tries to figure out what the war has done to him and his comrades. This is his conclusion: "We have become a waste-land. . . . Today we would pass through the scenes of our youth like travellers. We are burnt up by hard facts. . . . We are forlorn like children, and experienced like old men, we are crude and sorrowful and superficial—I believe we are lost. . . . Our knowledge of life is limited to death." And he concludes by likening his life to No-Man's-Land: "fields of craters within and without." This despair is no respecter of persons or flags. From the other side of the same battle lines, Vera Brittain in her *Testament of Youth* says that World War I condemned her and her generation to live to the end of their days "in a world without confidence, without security, a world in which every dear personal relationship would be fearfully cherished under the shadow of apprehension." It is this kind of despair which fastens itself upon the human spirit after it has been seared in the flames of war.

We are being told, and truly, I think, that "one of the biggest problems of our times is that of *degeneracy* stemming from despair." In brutal fact, how could it be otherwise? Did we think we could set the whole world to thinking war, talking war, planning war, and waging war without staggering moral and social reverberations? The worth of moral codes, along with the worth of human life, is challenged by the fact of killing which is the basic art, science, and aim of war. And what, concretely, has this meant? Immorality of every kind is increasing. An era of criminals is upon us. Laws are being broken. Conventions are being flouted. Another gin, jazz, and gangster era has come. Another "lost generation" is hunting through bizarre forms of literature and art in frantic search of its soul. Another generation of children born during these calamitous days is growing up in homes haunted by hunger, depression, despair, and fear for the future. The average age of the first offender in crime is dropping to a new low. Only a few years ago it was twenty years and over; now it is eighteen, and it is still dropping. Demagogues will soon arise in every area of life telling us of new "promised lands" to which they alone can lead us. And, because of our desire to escape the almost unendurable agony of apprehension and indecision that has followed this war, they will find many followers among us.

It is true, of course, that the widespread breakup of social and political patterns of life offers an unparalleled opportunity for rebuilding society on new and stabler foundations. Mr. John Foster Dulles, a well-known expert in international law, calls our attention to one marvelous vista of possibility: "It has been demonstrated, beyond doubt, that the old system of many disconnected sovereignties, each a law unto itself, inevitably breeds war. We must not keep humanity chained to such a wheel. Laying aside timidity, adding practicality to sentimentality, we must fearlessly plan a new world order." Of course, we should try to do just that. Courageous leaders like Mr. Dulles are, and will become even greater, towers of strength in the dark days that lie ahead. But an especial kind of suffering lies in store for us at precisely this point of need. The spiritual energies of many of us have been so completely depleted by the forces of cynicism, despair, and degeneracy that we simply will not try to answer the roll call for the new and greater cause. We will give it up as hopeless at the outset. We will console ourselves by saying, "You can't change human nature," and seek some corner where we can lick our wounds and snatch a moment of fitful peace before our part in the human drama is over. We will say with Edna St. Vincent Millay: *

> Let us abdicate now; let us
> Disintegrate quietly here,
> Convivially imbibing
> The pleasanter poisons.[2]

Spiritual exhaustion looms as a highly probable "journey's end" for most of us who are now being shaken by fits of righteous and self-righteous fury. And the newly born opportunity for reordering life and society will live for awhile in the minds and through the efforts of a few of God's noblemen, and then die for lack of sympathetic understanding and sacrificial support among

* *Conversation at Midnight.* Copyright, 1937, by Edna St. Vincent Millay.

the rank and file of mankind. And we and all that we hold dear will slip lower and lower in the descending spiral of catastrophe.

III

Against this background it is possible to summarize the various causes that underlie the spiritual ailments of our day.

First there is the sheer fact of irrevocable and irremediable loss. The recent war has robbed us of our best on every level of life. Its cost cannot be computed simply in terms of numbers of men, women, and children dead as a direct or indirect result of its activity—a number now upwards of fifty millions of persons. The number, of itself, is almost unbelievable, and the agony becomes unbearable as each number separates itself out of the total and, incarnate in the memory of a loved one, walks into our empty hearts and homes with a grief no words can catch. We must confront something more than the fact of fifty millions of people gone—tragic as that is. We must face the deeper fact that the two and one-half billions of people who remain are conscious of the absence of those who have gone, need their presence, and are keenly aware of the essential futility of their premature and violent departure.

Nor can we comprehend the meaning of the figure given as the financial cost of the war—five hundred eighty-six billions of dollars, as of V-J Day. Translated into human terms, it is enough to provide food, shelter, clothing, education, and health measures for all of the needy peoples of the world today and over the next half-century. It is enough to underwrite the cost of building a new economy in China and India, if not the entire Orient. Is it any wonder that we view the immediate past with mingled emotions of futility, disgust, and despair? And when men feel that way they are far down the road toward a serious spiritual ailment.

A second cause of our spiritual sickness is the shift in emphasis from the person to the group in contemporary culture. The group may be the community or the union or the church or the state. This depersonalization of life was well under way before the recent war struck, but the necessities of the total war accentuated it. Men became units in a military machine or numbers on the selective service board's list of manpower. Our sons were numbers in the service; if they were wounded or killed, they were casualties. The individuality of each one of us was haunted by that entity called the state which loomed over us all the time, determining what we wore, what we ate, where we went, and attentive to what we said. It controlled in large measure what we read, what we heard, what we wrote, and, as best it could, what we thought. To be sure, most of us were and are heartily sick of that kind of life and want to get as far away from it as possible.

But we are not likely to get far from it, try as we may. It had its good points and they are likely to seem better and better with each ensuing day of chaos and indecision in our internal economy as well as in international affairs. For one thing, it meant strength—the strength of a group. It meant security—one for all and all for one. It meant victory—the ability both to protect ourselves and to overthrow others. Soon after the demobilization program was well under way, a council of educators and clergymen was called by the Council on Higher Education to consider the problems of the educational outlook for veterans. Among those present were many soldiers both in and just out of service. During the discussion period a young man said, "As long as I was in the Army I was sure of three meals a day and a place to sleep and a little spending money. When I got my discharge, I kissed the Army good-by. I am out of the Army all right, but I am getting mighty worried about those meals and that spending money."

There, in a nutshell, is the problem at work in the minds of many today, making us double-business bound. Some are for pushing ahead toward the achievement of something we have never had before—a person-centered life and society. Others want to stick to the forms of collectivism and regimentation that have proved their worth in the recent past. Between the two a great argument is raging. Meantime, men grow hungry, restless, anxious—and wait, whether consciously or not, for some clear word from some strong leader. If the period of indecision is prolonged, we may be sure that that word will be spoken, and when it is, another Fuehrer will have come into existence.

A third reason for our spiritual plight is our loss of confidence in ourselves. Canon F. R. Barry says, "Christianity was born into a world that was haunted by the conviction that man was about played out." That comes close to being the perfect description of the deep feeling of pessimism which is plainly discernible these days. There is no way of dodging the fact that we are in a bad way. Nor is anything to be gained for good by disguising it behind a façade of pious wishes and hopes. The war ended with man playing god and making a ghastly mess of it. It ended with the realization that our scientific ability to create power has far outrun our moral ability to control it. It does seem that every good thing we create turns into a threat against our well-being. The eighteenth century could boast of man's reason and science, the nineteenth century of his industry, commerce, and a rising standard of living among many nations. The last half-century could boast of the rapid spread of learning and democracy in many sections of the world. But we know now that such boasts were premature. Such creations and achievements were and are good and valuable beyond all doubt, but, of themselves, they are not enough. Let them become infected with pride, greed, and selfishness—against which they seem to have no effective shield—and they become the instruments of greater evil than man ever dared dream he could engage in. Surrounded by the terror which these momentous achievements can bring to human life, man is asking, "Is everything we do infected with the germ of some fatal malady?"

New pessimism and despair are sweeping into the intellectual climate of Europe. For example, the most prominent philosopher in Paris just now is Jean-Paul Sartre, and his most widely read book is *The Philosophy of the Absurd*. This is the way the human situation looks to him: "We are isolated [from anyone else, from past and future, from even the past of ourselves], we are conscious of our own isolation, we make foolish and pathetic efforts to escape it. And the only remedy is Stoic courage." He continues his description of life and the world, "Man can will nothing unless he has first understood that he must count on no one but himself; that he is alone, abandoned on earth in the midst of his infinite responsibility, without help, with no other aims than the ones he sets himself, with no other destiny than the one he forges for himself on this earth." This being the case, "in such a world, it is difficult to posit values or a moral sense: all conduct will always be absurd in an absurd world, and we can decline all responsibility since our true Self does not belong to this world." Reasoning this way, Mr. Sartre is driven to the conclusion, "Life is absurd, love is impossible . . . all life is ambiguous, and there is no way of knowing the true meaning of what one is doing; perhaps even our actions have no meaning."[3] So we find ourselves ultimately condemned, according to the reasoning of this philosopher. Life is wholly meaningless. It has no center, no heart, no standard. It is hopelessly isolated from everything and everyone. We are separated from our self, our fellows, our God. We are really alone! There is no reality outside ourself that we can possibly touch. Small wonder he reaches the conclusion that moral endeavor on any other supposition than that of its absurdity is wholly worthless. One wonders what portent for the future of America lies in the fact that this philosopher is one of the first of the intellectual leaders of France to come to America in the postwar era.

A fourth reason for our spiritual illness is our fear for the future. An eminent scientist who had worked on the atomic bomb project said to me, "I'm scared to death by all this. Aren't you?" I answered, not wholly facetiously, "No, I can't say that I am. It is new to you but not to me. You see, you are a physicist, I am a theologian. We theologians have been looking into the throat of hell for two thousand years and you fellows have just found out there is such a place." If the war had ended by engendering a healthy fear of God in the hearts of men, it might conceivably have had some merit. But all it did was to create a great and paralyzing fear for the future in the hearts of everyone. We owe the great scientists of this country an unpayable debt for the evangelical zeal with which they are writing and speaking about the menace that looms over everyone and everything. Ten years ago only the pacifist would say, "There must be no more war." Now, scientists, educators, congressmen, and even presidents and prime ministers of the nations of the world are saying it. But fear of war is not enough to remove the threat of war—that ought to be plain to anyone. Fear of war actually slows down the speed necessary to develop a world organization which alone can stop war. If fear is to be conquered, the conqueror will not be more and greater fear, but something utterly different. It is at precisely this juncture that the Christian churches make a proposal for confronting the spiritual tragedy of our time. It is a proposition that every man who names the name of Christ study the meaning of being a Christian peacemaker and live as one. Before you, too, turn away sorrowing from this advice, which grows out of that given by the Great Physician long ago, consider what it means to be a Christian peacemaker.

IV

There is a fine story about the last days of George Lansbury, one of England's tireless workers for peace. He had spent all of his mature life wrestling with the knotty problems which lead to war. He lived through the First World War and died with the guns of the second one echoing through the world. It did seem like forty years thrown away! A close friend asked him how much nearer he thought peace was as a result of his efforts. Lansbury replied, "Forty years nearer!"

There's an antidote for the pessimism we so easily fall into about the inevitability of war, the hopelessness of peace! The spirit in Lansbury's reply brings sharply to mind the seventh beatitude or blessing of the Sermon on the Mount: "Blessed are the peacemakers: for they shall be called the children of God."

In a day when peacemakers are called pretty nearly everything else, it will repay and chasten us to inquire into the meaning which Jesus, in his teachings, pours into this beatitude.

Gerald Heard, in his book, *The Creed of Christ*, devotes a penetrating and suggestive chapter to this blessing. As you study his analysis you find yourself surrounded by a ring of probing questions. How many of us are qualified to be "peacemakers" as Christ seems to have meant the term? No one doubts our present fitness to wage war, but will anyone lay claim to the moral fitness to initiate peace, thought and action, as Christ understood them?

Obviously, before the Christian church can work effectively for a lasting peace it must be composed, more generally than it now is, of ministers and laity who will make a serious and sustained effort to be Christian peacemakers. That this type of competence requires more than superficial consent and verbal correctness will be abundantly clear as we study the four stages in the growth of the Christian peacemaker. As we move through them, ask yourself which one you are in at the present time. Or if you find that you are not in any of them, that you have not even made a start in the direction of becoming such a peacemaker, ask yourself, "What, in God's name, am I doing anyway that I think is more important?"

In the first stage of his growth, the Christian peacemaker *finds peace with God*. He accepts God as the basic Fact and Factor in human life and history. Whatever questions he has about God will fall within the circumference of confident faith in His reality. The inquiring mind will always be raising questions about God's meaning, will, or purpose. There is no other way to push back the horizons of our limited understanding and experience. There is no better way to pay tribute to the all-encompassing glory and richness of God than by determining, with Job-like stubbornness, to ask questions and to keep right on asking them until a reasonable answer is found. Finding God, so far from resolving all doubts and questions, actually stimulates them by making them useful and creative. They have in God a worthy Object, One in whose fuller truth they find their answer. To find peace with

God is to accept the further fact that "In his will is our peace," is to learn to say, "Not my will but Thine be done." To find God in this sense is to desire supremely to serve Him, to be willing to put first things first, to resolve to "seek first the Kingdom of God and His righteousness," knowing that all other needful things will be added.

Having found God in this profoundly personal sense, the Christian peacemaker moves imperceptibly into the second stage of growth, *one in which he finds peace with himself.* He lays a firm foundation for finding peace with himself by finding peace with God. He gives himself to God because that is the only sensible thing to do with his life. Simply to drift along without rhyme or reason, without purpose and plan is gross negligence. To deny that God has a claim on him, to assert that the Creator has no rights to or in His creature, to oppose His manifest will— this is sheer idiocy! The Christian peacemaker is driven to the ancient and humble confession: "Our hearts are restless until they rest in Thee."

With this decision, the Christian peacemaker's self ceases to be simply the plaything of desire and impulse and seeks to become the instrument of divine purpose and will. His life ceases to stew in the juices of words, fancies, and prejudices and is set to *work*, is absorbed in the *act*, the *deed*, is put on the *way*. In truth, the dynamic, on-going quality of life demands some such outlet in work in order to be wholesome, creative. Life never stands still. It is always going somewhere, somehow. It may be treading the high road of noble purpose and fine ideals, becoming, thereby, progressively richer and stronger. Or it may be taking the lower road of unguided impulse and ungoverned desire, becoming, thereby, progressively poorer and weaker. In the one case, life rises to new meanings; in the other, whatever meaning it has is slowly but surely debased and degraded.

The Christian peacemaker knows that, under God, the only way to keep himself from being a knot of frustrations, to keep his sanity as well as his spirituality, is to set himself to a mighty task. And, looking within himself as well as into the world of social relations, he sees no mightier task than that of peacemaking. But it will not be easy for the Christian peacemaker to find peace with himself. At least, this is the all but unanimous testimony of Christian history. The Gospel narratives, to cite but one instance, are dotted with people who could or would not find peace with themselves. Poor Judas is the extreme example. But for a long time in the life of stalwarts like Peter and Paul it looked as if he were going to have a lot of company! They too were known to kick against the pricks of God's will for them even after they knew what that will was! They were creatures of inconsistency and torment until they learned to say what a later hymn writer said, "Take my life and let it be consecrated, Lord, to Thee!" They finally learned to say it, finding grace and strength to humble their proud wills and spirits to the voice of God, thus finding peace with themselves.

The third stage in the growth of the Christian peacemaker is that in which he finds personal peace with others. Manifestly, there can be no such thing as complete peace with God and self when enmity toward others is raging, tornado-like, through our spirits. Jesus saw this and described what he saw in that sobering parable about who should and who should not approach God's altar with a gift. When a man is at peace with his brethren he may profitably place a gift on the altar. But if he "has aught against any man" he wastes his gift unless he puts it aside, while he makes peace with his brethren. This done, he may put the gift on God's altar.

The Christian peacemaker will *want* peace with others; he will take the initiative in peaceful attitudes and actions; he will risk rebuff; he will be prepared to fail; he will seek and find the strength to persist indefinitely until he is successful. He will strive for peace in the full sense of a mutual, two-way relationship of good will and understanding. Yet he knows that the possibility of failure to win this objective is always at hand. There is no way he can storm the citadel of another's soul. The wounds in the spirit of another may be too deep, too grievous, for any healing unguent he can place on them. But, even so, so far as it lies in the peacemaker's power he will have peace with even those who resist, rebuff, and seek to take advantage of him. If he cannot achieve peace in the full sense of a two-way relationship, he can do no less than make it a one-way affair. So far as his attitude toward others is concerned, to the extent that he can control his own tongue, his own actions, his own plans, he will "seek peace and pursue it." He knows that in this way he is making the supreme effort to overcome enmity; he knows, too, that it bears the seal of God's approval—which, for him, is enough.

In the likely event that others, in anger and greed, lay violent hands on him and seek to put him to death—even then his loyalty to peace does not succumb to the fear and anger which ignite as hatred and retaliation. Before you dismiss this as weakness, consider St. Francis' poignant parable of how the misunderstood and sadly mistreated Christian should greet each indignity. He should welcome it with the inner assurance that that is just what he deserves for having been so long blind to the glory of God, to the peace of Christ. The proud and powerful men of the day laughed at St. Francis' idea. They knew the "proper" way to deal with indignity and opposition! Yet when they by force of arms were unable to batter their crusade into Jerusalem, St. Francis, armed only with his meekness, walked through the battle lines and sought to persuade the sultan to become a Christian! Talk about courage and strength!

St. Francis' advice is not alien to the spirit of him who prayed in behalf of his persecutors, "Father, forgive them for they know not what they do." This spirit, and none other, will enable the Christian peacemaker to face any and every possible situation which may arise as he seeks peace with others.

The final stage in the growth of the Christian peacemaker is one in which he is equipped to be an instrument in peacemaking between others. By the time one has found peace with God, with himself, and with others, he will have acquired certain characteristics which are essential to this highest and hardest kind of peacemaking. He will be trusted by others because he is trustworthy. He will not be feared because of harm he can inflict since the entire set of his life will be against doing that. His word will be his bond; he will speak openly, honestly, and courageously; he will have none of the double talk which discourages friends and stimulates enemies. His motive in all his dealings with antagonists, be they persons or nations, will be that of finding *an enduring relationship* between them. He will not be the advocate of this person or nation against that person or nation; he will seek to be the advocate of justice and good will for all since these virtues alone bring peace.

The very integrity of the Christian peacemaker will be a danger to him because selfish, hateful men among the disputants will want to secure his name for their cause, will want him as a *front*, an *appearance* of virtue behind which they can mask and further their evil designs. Flattery, threats and solemn warnings will be used to cajole him into making "the worse appear the better cause." But he will have learned how to conquer similar tactics in his struggle for peace with himself and others. He will not succumb even though flattery, threats, and warning come to him in the guise of patriotism. His mission will be central in his life and mind—he is a peacemaker; by the mercy of God, he is a Christian peacemaker, one whose task it is to measure the contesting causes and claims by the mind of Christ, since there is no other sure road to permanent peace.

Now, quite obviously, the Christian peacemaker will not be permitted to intercede and institute the process of conciliation and reconciliation until the combatants have tried all known or available means of imposing their will on each other. But, finally, when the descending spiral of recurring conflicts reveals the pit of utter catastrophe into which both are falling, they may be willing to listen to what they have hitherto been content to reject as the counsel of perfection. There is reason to believe that the prospects of an atomic war have reduced contemporary civilization to some such state of moral desperation. After the last war, Lloyd George, powerful leader of a victorious nation, said, "The next great task of humanity is not deliverance by the sword, but deliverance from the sword." Arnold Toynbee's discussion of "The Saviour with the Sword" deserves to be studied by all who believe that we can guarantee peace by an overwhelming preponderance of military power. "The sword is only wielded in the hope of being able to use it to such good purpose that it may eventually have no more work to do; but this hope is an illusion; for it is only in fairyland that swords cut Gordian knots which cannot be untied by fingers. 'All they that take the sword shall perish with the sword' is the inexorable law of real life; and the swordsman's belief in a conclusive victory is an illusion. . . . The Saviour with the sword may perhaps build a house upon the sand but never the house upon a rock." [4]

But, thank God, not many people are honestly prepared to stake the future of our civilization on force of arms. They will do so only as a last resort, for it is pitifully plain to all that wars are social earthquakes which no one wins. If the common man accepts war as inevitable, the blame will lie squarely on us who desire to be known as Christians but will not make the effort to be Christian peacemakers! There rests upon us the infinite obligation to discover and explore all possibilities for peace in the concrete conflicts which are now raging. "Blessed are the peacemakers for they shall be called the children of God."

But, you object, none of us are or ever will be peacemakers in the full and complete sense of being a Christian peacemaker. It's too hard, too exacting for mortal man! It's impossible!

Not many will think that the supreme gift of being a child of God would be given us for the asking. The supreme achievement open to man requires nothing less than the supreme efforts of a lifetime. Only the man who has tried it with his whole soul has a right to say that it is impossible to be a Christian peacemaker. And, let it be noted, the ones, like George Lansbury, who earn the right to answer it assure us that, with all its enormous difficulties, the task of Christian peacemaking is possible, and it alone is hopeful.

Actually, we have no way of knowing how good a Christian peacemaker we can become until and unless we devote the best efforts of a lifetime to it. This means finding peace with God, with ourselves, with others, before we are equipped to be an instrument in peacemaking between others. These four stages of growth are tied together like infancy, childhood, youth, maturity. They are related to one another as the base and peak of a pyramid are related to each other. Neither, by itself, is or can ever be a pyramid. So it is with Christian peacemaking. Beginning with the broad foundation of peace with God, we toil upward stone by stone until finally we aspire to be a humble but willing instrument of God's will, a child of God, in the work of establishing "peace on earth, good will among men." We must be willing to say: "I propose, under God, to labor at the whole structure, limited only by my ability and opportunity." We must forswear the temptation to measure ourselves by any other standard than that of "the mind of Christ." This temptation will beset us daily, hourly, not only from without but even more desperately from within. We will want some lower, some easier, some more convenient standard. Appalled by the task before us, dismayed by our failures, our inadequacy, we will be tempted to make more convenient gods in our own image, rather than brave the miracle of creation of being remade in the image of God. But the price of idolatry continues to be spiritual death while the reward of true religion is strength and peace.

V

Let it be underscored, then, that Christian men and women cannot stand idly by while the disintegrative forces of the day reach, like a sword, into our standards, our homes, and our whole society. Christian homes, as they cherish their faith, will get a new grip on the spiritual resources of fellowship and trust. They will seek to be islands of complete understanding and sympathy in a world in which men are being forced to grapple with mistrust and hatred. Christian churches must not forget their mission—the proclamation of the gospel. This is a *world* mission. Our hardest task is now at hand—preaching the gospel of love

and brotherhood in a world either at war or filled with the
hatreds bred of war. There is no occasion for self-pity in that.
Our task is no more hopeless than that which has confronted
the church in many earlier periods. We bear in our body the
scars which were their wounds. The Cross will slip into the
focus of our thinking as the only adequate and relevant Christian
symbol for such trials of men's souls. As persons seeking to be
Christians in our living, no one will need to urge us to a deeper
consecration of ourselves to the Christian way of life as we see
it in the life and teachings of Jesus Christ. Out of this experience
of humble, sincere, and persistent dedication to him will flow
hope, courage, and purpose sufficient unto even this day.

Consider, then, these manifold tasks: tireless efforts toward
permanent peace; the determination to keep alive a fellowship
of faith in mankind; the insistent obligation to face the future
in terms of a vital faith in God as we see Him in Jesus Christ.
This is our work and we ought to be doing it. It constitutes the
Christian approach to the tragedy of suffering. And when Christian churches appeal to men and women like us to carry on in
these undertakings they are making their supreme effort to alter
the tragic ending which is fast closing in on the drama of our
day. The Christian gospel is not man-made, but it becomes intelligent, resourceful, and desperately relevant only insofar as persons neither wiser nor better than we are yield themselves to its
transforming power.

When we waver at the very great probability that what we
are trying to do will be tossed aside as irrelevant by an action-
crazed world, we need to remind ourselves that "Except a grain
of wheat fall into the ground and die, it abideth alone, but if it
die it bringeth forth much fruit." When we are tempted to give
it up in despair, we need to remember that Christians before us
have faced with courage the sunset of their civilization, and that
we follow One of whom it has been truly said, "He turned their
sunsets into sunrises." When we stumble, as stumble we will,
through blindness, new courage can come flooding in from the

comradeship of him who came "feeding sunshine to the blind." There is no sword known to man that can sever this faith of ours in the living God—but it can be surrendered. We are the only ones that can do that.

Chapter II ❧※ SKEPTICISM KNOWS
NO ANSWER

I

James Gordon Gilkey tells of a college student who
put a question mark in the vacant niche of a Gothic chapel on
a certain campus. His companion asked him what that meant.
"That is for God," was the earnest and grim reply. That young
man engaged in putting symbols of doubt in places reserved for
symbols of faith is himself an all too apt symbol of the spiritual
climate of these days. Until and unless we can find the will and
the way to transform such skepticism into great faith, we shall
not be prepared for the enormous tasks which engage our attention in the world at large.

When people say, "I am a skeptic," one of three things is
usually true: (1) They do not know what they are saying; (2)
they do not actually mean what they say; or (3) they both know
and mean what they say and thereby place themselves almost
beyond the hope of spiritual redemption. The seriousness of
these alternatives is dictated by the simple fact that skepticism
is one of the most dangerous attitudes of mind and spirit a human
being can conceivably embrace. It can and it will snap the nerve
of vital thought and vigorous action quicker than any other
known attitude. A generation "sicklied o'er with the pale cast"
of skeptical thought is an easy and ready prey for any militant
minority that comes marching and singing into its stagnant spiritual life. Amiel, the Swiss philosopher-mystic, lifts a word of
warning that is as timely today as ever: "The unbelieving epochs
are the cradles of new superstitions."

Skepticism always fishes in troubled waters. It has its best luck when disillusionment and anxiety disturb the spirits of men. It offers, or seems to offer, an easier alternative than that of facing the situation squarely and seeing it through as a thoroughly responsible person. Which, more than anything else, accounts for the fact that skepticism is always on the upswing in postwar days. When the hopes and ideals that seemed to be near at hand in the war are dashed to earth by the uncertainties of the ensuing period of uneasy peace, the spirit of man wearies to the point of complete exhaustion. If there is any way other than that of groping forward step by step through an indefinitely long future, we are tempted to investigate it. Skepticism offers such a short cut; that is why it is an ever growing menace today; that is why thoughtful people need to pay it the honor of understanding what it is, what its proposals for life are. It will then be plain why vital religion always greets skepticism with a challenge to mortal combat. They are truly irreconcilable; between them a man must choose. He cannot serve disbelief and belief at one and the same time.

In talking about skepticism, or any other high theme, it is particularly important to know as precisely as possible from the very outset what is meant by the crucial term. This is but to heed Paul's warning to all vigorous champions of the faith, "So fight I as not to fight the air." As we study skepticism in theory and in practice it will be clear that to lay down a challenge to it is not to fight the air. To close with skepticism is to be pitted against one of the most persistent and implacable enemies known to the human spirit.

II

Skepticism, in theory, is too complex a thing to be caught in the net of a single definition. The *Dictionary of Philosophy* [1] distinguishes the following meanings that, at various times, are carried by the term: (1) It is the assertion that, for one reason or another, the human mind is incapable of getting reliable knowledge about such ultimate matters as "God, one's self, other selves, and values . . ."; (2) it is the insistence that the best and only reliable method of seeking knowledge is to doubt the validity of any given proposition "until something indubitable or as nearly indubitable as possible is found"; until such evidence is forthcoming "judgment should be suspended"; (3) it is the claim "that morality is entirely a matter of individual preference," that there is no ultimate moral nature in life and the universe to which our moral ideals and efforts need to conform; (4) it is an attitude of disbelief ranging through several possible forms: (a) "an attitude involving no greater inclination to belief than to disbelief nor to disbelief than belief"; (b) an attitude involving greater inclination to disbelief than belief"; (c) "an attitude of complete or dogmatic disbelief"; (5) it is the proposal that self-ishness is the mainspring in human conduct, that sincerity, al-truism, and any other higher motives are ineffectual; there is, therefore, no reason to believe in the ultimate "worth or hope of success of any one or all of man's enterprises."

One need not be a professional philosopher to see why skep-ticism, so conceived, is at immediate and irreconcilable logger-heads with religious faith. Turn each one of these possible meanings over in your mind slowly and you will readily under-stand why religion will neither ask nor give quarter to skepticism in their inescapable encounter. What it means to laymen is blood brother to what it means to experts. As embraced or en-countered by ordinary people, *skepticism means an attitude of disbelief in the reality of God and the trustworthiness of man.* Skepticism substitutes chance for design, impression for knowl-edge, accident for purpose, despair for hope, and loneliness for love. In its milder form, it results in an agnosticism which con-tents itself with saying, "I do not know whether there is a being corresponding to the word 'God.' The evidence is far from fin-ished or incomplete. Therefore, I refuse either to say or to live as though there were a God." Turning to man, agnosticism continues, "Neither do I know whether human nature is essen-tially trustworthy. Some men are and many are not. I propose to be dubious about all men until they prove their worth."

In its extreme form skepticism becomes atheism, and flatly says,

"I find no reason for believing in the reality of God or the reliability of man. Therefore I disbelieve in them and propose to live accordingly." The implications of theoretical skepticism for religious faith are plain enough. Dr. Rufus M. Jones points them up fairly: "There is no future for religion, no permanence to its inspiration and lifting power, unless men and women—and the children who share their outlook and their ideals—can continue genuinely and sincerely to believe in God as the ground and reality of that which is good, the spring and basis of a real moral and spiritual universe, the life and inspiration of all our aims at righteousness and truth, the Great Companion Who shares with us in the travail and tragedy of the world and Who is working through us to 'bring things up to better.' " [2] Let skepticism go unchallenged and it will drive the keen edge of doubt not alone between man and God but also between man and man and between man and the worth-whileness of life itself. Actually, this is what happens when skepticism gets loose in the life of a man or a people. In practice, it proposes a radically different kind of living from that recommended by vital religion. Just how different may be glimpsed in two incidents drawn from the Bible.

The Seventy-third Psalm was written by a man who was deeply perplexed by the apparent contradiction between religion's claim that this world is under the reign of God and the real fact of the prosperity of the wicked and the suffering of the righteous. He wrestled with the problem of how these things could be in God's world and could find no satisfactory answer. But the prosperous and proud skeptics of his day had an answer that suggested a way out of his difficulty. They asked, "How doth God know? And is there knowledge in the Most High?" Which amounts to saying, "If there is a God at all, He either does not know or does not care about what happens in the affairs of men." This doubt pushed and shoved at the Psalmist's faith until "his steps had well nigh slipped." Fortunately, a mystical experience of the reality of God steadied him and enabled him to keep on the highway of faith. But when it looked as if skepticism would win out, the Psalmist saw clearly that he would have to be ready to abandon the way of life based upon belief and trust in the goodness of God. That is the practical meaning of skepticism—not a new way of thinking but a new way of living, one in which old standards and goals are disavowed and new ones exalted. It is, in effect, conversion in reverse, conversion away from the will of God rather than to it.

Pilate (more to be pitied than condemned) furnishes, in the one episode of his life that found its way into history, another illustration of skepticism's proposal for life. Like all educated Romans of the day, especially those in positions of official responsibility in the provinces adjacent to the Mediterranean, Pilate had heard truth discussed by the wisest men of the three great civilizations that clustered on the shores of that fabulous sea: Roman, Greek, and Hebrew. He was impressed with the wide disagreements which cropped up in these discussions. As a result, he seems to have reached the conclusion that the quest for truth is all but hopeless. So he became a skeptic, doubting the reality of anything beyond the Roman Empire and deeper than the Roman law. He accepted these as moral ultimates, deriving his course of action from them and defining himself in terms of them. We know too little about him to say that his skepticism was thoroughgoing enough to question their validity. What we do know leads us to believe that they were the nearer gods of his life. Like many other skeptics, he seems to have combined a basic skepticism about God and man with a strong enough provisional conviction about duty to enable him to be one of Caesar's most acceptable governors.

This combination of skepticism and limited conviction helped him out of a tight spot when Jesus of Nazareth was brought before him by the irate leaders of the influential Jewish circles in Jerusalem. Although the charges against Jesus were clearly religious in nature, his accusers were demanding the death penalty —an extremity which could be ordered by Pilate himself. Pilate heard their case and saw at once that it had no foundation in fact for presentation in his court. He could have dismissed it and them forthwith, but he hesitated to do so. It would mean more trouble for him; it would mean one more grievance against his administration that would find its way into any bill of complaints that might be forwarded to his superiors. Pilate sought an easy way out of the impasse. He questioned Jesus about the charges, particularly his reported claim to be the King of the Jews. Jesus seems to have admitted the claim but said that his kingship was not of this world. Pilate laughingly asked, "So you are a King?" There was neither merriment nor shame in Jesus' reply, "For this I was born, and for this I have come into the world, to bear witness to the truth. Everyone who is of the truth hears my voice." Pilate, speaking the eternal text of skepticism asked, "What is the truth?"

That was more, tragically more, than an idle or theoretical inquiry. Do you recall what Pilate did immediately after making it? Heeding the artificial slogans of a paid mob, he condemned an admittedly innocent man to death as a criminal and released an admitted criminal in his stead! That is precisely the kind of moral situation which lies beyond the door of skepticism now as then. Skepticism enabled Pilate to sidestep an unpleasant situation without too much prodding from his conscience. It provided a dodge around a concrete issue in which the rights of one man were set over against the wishes of many, and between them Pilate was forcd to choose. He made his choice—the kind of choice you can make without too much uneasiness of mind and conscience if you are a skeptic, if you think you live in a world where God does not matter, where human life is a cheap and relatively unimportant part of the scheme of things, where moral responsibility for the lives and welfare of others can be assumed or dodged at will and without remorse.

But why hurdle nineteen centuries in search of the fruits of skepticism in human life and affairs? By any manner of reckoning, skepticism is one of the principal authors of one of the most wretched chapters in human history—the last half-century. We of all people should know the human meaning of disbelief in the reality of God and the trustworthiness of man. It has fought steadily for the domination of our mind, spirit, and way of life. Most of us have matured in an age of out-and-out skepticism, one which led or tried to lead us to believe that what we think about God is a marginal matter—an intellectual luxury, if you please. Our spiritual plight is well expressed by an incident in Howard Spring's *My Son, My Son*. The agents are oppressed by premonitions of the doom which is closing in upon them. Someone recalls wistfully how God intervened to save Isaac from the sacrificial knife of Abraham. Then Maeve, for whom life had once been so hopeful and was now so hopeless, says, "Good old God! Can you see him intervening today? I can't!" Neither could anyone else! There the matter was left. And there it remained not alone for them but for most of our generation until almost yesterday: God—a good idea but with no foundation in fact; God—all right for an earlier day, perhaps, but with absolutely no relevance to our own. Skepticism like this took fast hold of the Western world following the First World War. And it was no mere intellectual fad! It was a grim fact that worked itself into the very fabric of human life and affairs. When we lost faith in the reality of God, we lost faith in the reliability of men. Our fears rather than our faith became the cruel determiners of our destiny. And not of ours only but of our children's also through an unpredictably long future. For these parent fears were so widespread, so real, that they contributed materially to the defeat of every attempt to rebuild the shattered structure of Western civilization.

Dr. C. J. Hambro, Norwegian delegate to the League of Nations and the last president of the Assembly of that body, wrote its epitaph as early as 1935 when he said, "Here in Geneva we have every fear but the fear of God!" This is the most profound explanation I have yet seen of why the League failed. Historians indicate the two or three crucial problems in which the League failed and because of which its power waned. That, of course, is both true and important in any appraisal of its work. But the fundamental fact remains that what actually killed the League was the atmosphere of distrust in which it was forced to carry on its work for peace. Fear of and for markets and industries, fear of other nations (always taking them at their worst and thus encouraging the worst in them)—this was the blanket of skepticism which suffocated not only the League's efforts for peace but the League itself.

One of the most penetrating descriptions of the root-cause of the chaos of the twenties and thirties was contributed by a disillusioned German writer, "The benevolent Father God of pre-war Europe was the first fatality of that conflict." Well, if He was the first fatality, Western civilization was the second, and, unless we are wiser than we seem, mankind itself will be the third!

Why war sires skepticism is not difficult to understand. War is the complete inversion of the values by which we seek to live in time of peace. Virtues become vices and vices virtues. We know now that it is far easier to destroy than to construct a system of values. We ought to understand the Chinese description of a toboggan slide: "Psst—and walk back!" It takes longer than one generation to recover from the spiritually devastating experience of saying—and trying to believe—that black is white and white is black. To live through this experience—and we have had a double dose of it—is to place a question mark after every affirmation and affirming agency known to man. This is the human meaning of skepticism, and it follows war as surely as night follows day.

Not only was skepticism an active factor in preventing the rebuilding of the world after the First World War; it set the stage for the cataclysmic destruction of the next war. Herman Rausching's book, *The Revolution of Nihilism*, ought to be required reading these days when we are trying to recover from one war and to avert another. Writing in 1937-38 he said ". . . It must be recalled that the world of ideas of the nationalist, conservative, and liberal middle class and aristocracy, and of the intellectuals, had long been invaded by skepticism." [3] He gives this word of warning to all groups today when he says that the real weakness of one of the potential enemies of Hitler's rise to power, the Monarchist group, lay in ". . . its complete skepticism as to the relevance of spiritual and moral forces to practical politics." [4] William Henry Chamberlin may well have had the period between the wars in mind when he said that "one of the most appalling aspects of the modern world is the breakdown of absolute moral values." [5]

Against this background it is easier to understand the prairie-fire suddenness of the Nazi rise to power. It swept into lives that were organized around a spiritual vacuum instead of a great faith. It confronted leaders in business, government, and intellectual life who had translated their skepticism into opportunism. They were willing to ride the winds that promised to lift the highest. Although they professed not to be taken in by "the fanaticism" of the Nazi leaders, they were impressed by the power of the party—so along they went on what must be regarded as a most disastrous ride.

Then came the dread day of reckoning for skepticism as an active force in the life of the German people. Instead of being grateful for its effective work as spiritual saboteur and rewarding it with high praise and a high place, the new gods of blood, soil, and race would have none of it. What it had done to the gods it might do to the half-gods! So they swept it out at once and demanded of its erstwhile exponents an intensity of loyalty, belief, and sacrificial service equaled only by the most fanatical periods in religion's long history. Like Haman of old, skepticism erected the gallows for the execution of religion's faith in God and man only to die itself thereon.

Skepticism suffered a similar fate in other parts of the Western world. Most of us can recall the mass conversion of cynics into crusaders during the early days of the recent war. Literary lights like Ernest Hemingway and Robert Sherwood once asked, "What is truth?" Life to them was a question mark, and sacrificial devotion to great ideals a laugh. So far from being alone, they were simply two of the most effective leaders of the literary clans wandering in the wastelands of skepticism. "Our task," they said, "is to note problems." This they did with superb artistry. But there they stopped because there the trail ended—or so they thought! One of their number, Archibald MacLeish, looking back on that period of cynical indecision or decisive doubt dubs himself and his colleagues "The Irresponsibles" because he feels that they undermined our faith in the democratic way of life, in the essential goodness of man, and in the possibility of a hopeful future in human history.

But, as always happens, life shouldered the skeptics roughly ahead into an ominous and tragic future. They were confronted by the necessity of living intensely, passionately, with an unbelievable wholeness of mind and integrity of spirit and doing so with some kind of faith or other!

Mr. Robert Sherwood is an apt symbol of what took place. Under the full moon of skepticism he had written *Idiot's Delight* —an unforgettable etching of the inability of any creative loyalty to weather the storm of war. Mr. Sherwood has no answer to this tragic fact. He simply notes it with poignant regret and consummate dramatic art. But when the war actually came, some answer had to be found that tried to make sense of the war. Mr. Sherwood wrote a second play, *There Shall Be No Night*. It pictures the agonized struggle of a sensitive spirit that hates war, that disbelieves in it, yet feels forced by world events into a decision to fight for the attempted preservation of those very loyalties that war is almost certain to wreck. But this, surely, is not skepticism. It is great conviction! For now there are loyalties worth living and dying for even though the chance of guaranteeing their triumph is exceedingly slender.

Overnight our skeptics became prophets. They raised banners and chanted slogans calculated to stir people into decisive, vigorous action. All pretense of objectivity was abandoned; lines were drawn and men confronted with the challenge, "Who is on the Lord's side, let him come to me. . . ." They deified "democracy" or "our way of life" or "freedom" and erected altars "on every high hill and under every green tree" and demanded that men place their lives thereon as votive offerings.

In simple fact it could not be otherwise. There is no place for skepticism in mortal combat. It has been demonstrated over and over again that you cannot wage a war without the irreplaceable strength of at least a quasi-religious fervor behind and within both sides. A really great war must be regarded as "a holy war" before men will live and die sacrificially for its prosecution. Let us give the devil his just due, then, in this and every other case: skepticism is distinguished by its ability to produce but its utter inability to wage a war. It can and does clear the way for war by undermining our belief in and loyalty to the reality of God and the trustworthiness of men. This done, each fraction of mankind is ready to lift its banner of race or nation or class or creed and make war upon all others, if need be. Amiel was surely right! For out of the unbelieving epoch which followed the First World War sprang the superstitions which not only disowned skepticism but actually raced madly on into the Second World War.

III

I am choosing my words carefully when I say that skepticism is a lost cause if ever there was a lost cause in the history of thought and life. In an age when men are once more being tempted to follow it into the wastelands of confusion, frustration, and, ultimately, over the brink of ruin itself, the futility, the utter inadequacy, the profound lostness of skepticism need to be impressed upon everyone. Men need to know that it is a lost cause; lost intellectually, socially, and spiritually.

Skepticism is a lost cause intellectually for the simple reason that it can no longer find champions in any of the great disciplines of the human mind. Time was—and in the recent past— when it could find representatives among the best minds in science and philosophy. Modern philosophy was oriented mainly to the methods and principles of what Sir James Jeans has called "classical mechanism" in science throughout the nineteenth century and the first two decades of the twentieth. A reliable historian of that period gives this picture of the resulting world view: "In all the reaches of our telescopes and microscopes there is nowhere discoverable the slightest trace of anything like man, any friend behind phenomena, any God who cares, any principle that guarantees man's success in his struggles and endeavors. So far as the eye of science can see, man is alone, absolutely alone, in a universe in which his very appearance is a kind of cosmic accident." [6] In many ways Mr. Bertrand Russell's *Sceptical Essays* [7] and "A Free Man's Worship" [8] appear to bring to a climax this long period when skepticism seemed the inevitable and final journey's end of reason.[9] That, however, proved not to be the case. Scientists and philosophers alike have now generally renounced that conclusion. In fact, they are taking the lead in bringing the whole position of skepticism under a hot fire of criticism. They are doing this not because of any new-found interest in religion but because certain revolutionary developments in scientific theory and principles have seriously curtailed the usefulness of the whole notion of mechanism. It is no longer possible for one to reduce all events to the formula of "mass in motion."

Sir James Jeans devotes an entire chapter in his recent book, *Physics and Philosophy*,[10] to "The Passing of the Mechanical Age." And with its passing there disappeared the foundation for the philosophy of determinism which visualized the universe as being, basically, particles controlled by rigid mathematical laws and which had, therefore, no place for any event which might stem from the free activity of God or the free will of man. So long as a mechanistic determinism was in the saddle of man's mind, philosophy was in the service of skepticism. But determinism departed precipitously with two discoveries: [11] (1) the discovery of what has been called three new worlds—the world of the nebulae, the world of the electron, and the world of man; (2) the discovery that while the principles of mechanistic scientific theory continue to throw some light on the world of man, they are utterly inadequate for the new worlds. Laplace, the French scientist at the beginning of the nineteenth century, gave it as his opinion "That if the state of the world at its creation were specified in its minutest detail to an infinitely capable and infinitely industrious mathematician, such a being would be able to deduce the whole of its subsequent history. 'Nothing would be uncertain for him; the future as well as the past would be present to his eyes.' " [12] I do not know of a single scientist today who could say that or anything like it. The difference between the "then" and the "now" has been so well stated by Sir James Jeans that it deserves to be quoted in full: "The classical physics seemed to bolt and bar the door leading to any sort of freedom of the will; the new physics hardly does this; it almost seems to suggest that the door may be unlocked—if only we could find the handle. The old physics showed us a universe which looked more like a prison than a dwelling-place. The new physics shows us a universe which looks as though it might conceivably form a suitable dwelling-place for free men, and not a mere shelter for brutes—a home in which it may at least be possible for us to mould events to our desires and live lives of endeavor and achievement." [13]

The scientist, as a rule, does not get excited when you doubt the theological refinements of the idea of God, but he girds on his armor in a hurry when you say you can dispense with the entire meaning of the reality of God. He can no more do his work without the concept of order, for example, than can a theologian. For the scientist believes that there is an objective order in the world. The purpose of his experiments is to discover the fuller meaning of that order. The word "verification," which is the watchdog of scientific conclusions, and the word "discovery," which is the spur of scientific endeavor, depend for their meaning upon the reality of the orderliness of the universe. Modern science has advanced far beyond the simple ideas of order with which it began its career, but it has not forsaken and dares not forsake the notion of order itself. It has been forced to develop a number of principles that would startle Galileo, Kepler, and Newton, viz., the principle of discontinuity, of uncertainty, and of probability. The very existence of these is eloquent testimony to the fact that the orderliness of the universe as discovered is proving to be an evasive and complex reality.

Small wonder Max Planck, one of the greatest modern scientists, was of the opinion that these words ought to be engraved over each laboratory: "Ye must have faith!" It is the emergence of this spirit of humility and reverence in the presence of both the definiteness and the mystery of the universe that has led most scientists out of the ranks of the skeptics into the ranks of men who believe that:

> This world's no blot for us,
> Nor blank; it means intensely and means good;
> To find its meaning is my meat and drink.[14]

Not all scientists would go the whole distance with Gorge Washington Carver: "I discover nothing in my laboratory. If I come here of myself I am lost. But I can do all things through Christ. I am God's servant, His agent, for here God and I are alone. I am just the instrument through which He speaks, and I would be able to do more if I were to stay in closer touch with Him. With my prayers I mix my labors, and sometimes God is pleased to bless the result." [15] But very few would disagree with Einstein: "Science without religion is lame, and religion without science is blind." [16]

Nor is skepticism faring much better among the philosophers just now. A thoroughgoing skeptic is and has always been a rare bird in that company. Yet, strangely, many a layman is of the opinion that skepticism is practically synonymous with philosophy. The cautious, questioning method by which philosophy proceeds may explain some of this misunderstanding. Philosophy does proceed slowly because she must keep a careful eye on known facts; she is as eager to hear the testimony of a doubt as an affirmation, since either may lead to new discoveries of truth. Her interest in knowledge makes her test every opinion, and her concern for truth leads her to examine every claim with every test she knows. To put it briefly, what many people mistake for skepticism is simply philosophy's determination to keep faith with the fact of our ignorance. She does not say we cannot achieve reliable knowledge of reality; rather, she devotes her efforts to an appraisal of the degree of truth in our various claims to knowledge. Essentially, then, philosophy is a critical rather than a skeptical discipline.[17]

From the days of Socrates and Plato the skeptic has received hard words when his case has come up before the vast majority of the creative thinkers of the Western World. Plato was frankly impatient and openly intolerant of men who doubted the reality of God.[18] In fact, he was upset by the necessity of even matching arguments with them. "Who can be calm when he is called upon to prove the existence of the Gods? Who can avoid hating and abhorring the men who have been the cause of this argument . . . ?" "The reality of the Gods," he contends, "would be admitted by all who had any particle of intelligence. . . ." He asks, ". . . How can any one in gentle terms remonstrate with the like of them . . . ?" But he recognizes that the reality of the gods must be accepted if law, morality, and society are to have any form or future. Thereupon he launches into his best discussion of the meaning of God and His relevance to the affairs of men. Plato does not let skeptics off with merely an intellectual battle. They are much too dangerous, he thinks, to be permitted to run loose in the common life. He feels that men should be persuaded to respect God if possible. If not, they deserve to be punished with the punishment suited to the crime. Innocent offenders—those whose disbelief rests on what others have told them—are to be imprisoned until they come to their senses. More serious offenders—those who hold their atheism with wholehearted conviction—are to be executed. The most serious offenders of all, "those who believe that the gods favor the wicked in return for their gifts shall be imprisoned during life, and never again hold intercourse with their fellows, and when they die, their bodies shall be cast beyond the borders."

Francis Bacon draws up an equally heavy indictment of the skeptic: "They that deny a God, destroy man's nobility; for clearly man is of kin to the beasts by his body, and if he be not of kin to God by his spirit, he is a base and ignoble creature." Although we may hesitate to subscribe to the line of reasoning which Bacon uses, there is no doubt that he is convinced of its validity and is prepared to enforce it with every power at his disposal. Yet Bacon is one of the patron saints of the entire empirical and pragmatic movement—the fact-minded movement—in modern philosophy. It never occurred to him, as it has to some of his successors, that the reality of God can be doubted either easily or successfully. The order and system which science encountered in the universe was, to him, evidence of structure and design, and these, in turn, bespoke the existence of a Being, God.

Immanuel Kant could and did place a question mark over most of the knowledge-claims which man made about God. He studied the most widely used theological and philosophical proofs for the existence of God and declared them worthless. Heine says that Kant was worse than Robespierre, who had killed a king and a few thousand Frenchman "while Kant had killed God, had undermined the most precious arguments of theology." [19] Although traditional theologians and philosophers regarded him as "the great destroyer," actually Kant was bent on proving the reality of God and felt he had to dispose of the wrong ways of doing it before he could embark upon the right one. His own way lay through accepting the reality of moral sense and the moral law. These, he argued, are indubitable parts of human experience. This being true, and he spends most of a long book (Critique of Practical Reason) pointing out that it is, there are certain implications that not only may but must be drawn. And when Kant had finished drawing them he was in possession of what he regarded as proof of the freedom of the will, immortality, and God. The reality of the moral law is guaranteed by our moral sense, he reasons, and carries with it as an inescapable implication the acceptance of the existence of God, freedom, and immortality. If it is true that Kant outskepticked the skeptics of his day, it is equally true that he outtheologized the theologians.

Very few, if any, of our contemporary philosophic leaders will submit to classification as skeptics. Even Bertrand Russell and John Dewey have a frame of cosmic reference for life and thought that, at many points, is not unlike religion's faith in God and man. Although both would hesitate to let the word "God" be applied to this frame of reference because, to them, it is not personal in structure or activity, they do gain a real sense of dependability for living and working from it. Order, system, form— these are essential attributes of the universe as experienced and discovered, say these thinkers. Our ideals are not alien importations in the universe, says Dr. Dewey. They are as much a part of nature as man himself is and are to be accepted as real, dependable approaches to and interpretations of the essential nature of life and reality. Dr. Dewey's *A Common Faith* is a restrained and cautious (overly so, some think) statement of a vital religious position which is worlds removed from skepticism. Other philosophic giants—A. N. Whitehead, John Elof Boodin, Edgar Brightman, S. Alexander—are open and avowed theists. While their thought, like Kant's, gives traditional-minded theists unhappy moments, it provides nothing but sweeping condemnation for skepticism. The universe as known and experienced is the scene of activity which deserves the name of will, purpose, and being. Such men stand up quickly to be counted among those who affirm the reality of God and the trustworthiness of man.

Skepticism is a lost cause intellectually because it plainly is a parasite which, having no self-sustaining life of its own, depends for its livelihood upon its ability to attach itself to a healthy affirmation or creed. To say this is not to ignore the creative role of doubt and persistent questioning in the development of truth in any area of life. But, even here, major emphasis must fall upon the importance of the truth rather than some part of the method by which it is reached. Skepticism about the validity of Ptolemaic astronomy undoubtedly spurred Galileo into his famous experiments, but his experiments were epoch making because they disclosed a solid truth about reality. The main thrusts of the creative disciplines of the human mind—science, philosophy, art, theology —are toward achievement of a body of affirmations, a system of truth, an enduring insight into the nature of reality.

Skepticism is a lost cause socially both in principle and in practice. It is lost in principle because it ignores or denies the fundamental role played by trust and confidence in the growth of human personality and in the structure of any enduring social group. Personality has been defined as "the possibility of mirroring God, the faculty of being a living reflection of the very attributes and character of the Most High." That is what personality means for faith, but not for skepticism!

Lying at the center of the human personality is that mysterious yet dynamic and definite entity known as "self." While students of human nature dispute loud and long about the meaning and characteristics of the self (some wanting to strip it of practically all meaning, others wanting to endow it with all that is to develop later), there is unanimity on this point: the most important characteristic of the self is its potential for interrelatedness. It is endowed with countless numbers of arms, as it were, reaching out to link it in new ways with the surrounding world. A child's eagerness for new experiences, its avid curiosity in the presence of that which is novel, its love of that which is familiar—these are "outward and visible signs" of the "inner and spiritual" reality of growing selfhood. With adolescence and maturity capacities for new forms of interrelatedness emerge, and, as they form the basis of actual relationships, the self shares in the creation of new meanings which are bonds between it and its total world.

The ideal environment for the growth of personality would be one in which trust and confidence were normal attitudes for the child to take toward others and toward new experiences. These are the creative, the outreaching attitudes whereby the self grows in the number and meaning of its interrelationships. They are as necessary for maturity as for infancy and adolescence since they spell the difference between the expansive and the contractive personality.

The expansive personality is one in which the self moves outward, eager to meet and understand other people with friendliness, glad to co-operate with them. If yours is an expansive personality, you are not afraid to leave the home base of the things you are sure of and move into the unknown with real confidence. The contractive personality pretty generally reverses this pro-

cedure. You stand within the center of self and continually draw
in the horizons of your responsibility. You try to be self-con-
tained and self-sufficient. You strive to create a little cell of security around yourself—there to live and there to die.

This, in all too brief form, is an abstract picture of the way in
which the human personality grows, or tries to grow, to the realization of its capacities. Throughout, it is a matter of acquiring
new meanings for self by accepting new bonds with others. If
at any point in the process the self begins to retreat from new
relationships, not only is its grow arrested at that point but, actually, a disintegrating process sets in, by virtue of which the
self is slowly stripped of meaning and of its consciousness of
worth. The lost soul might be defined as a self that has tried to
save itself by severing all meaningful relationships with others.
Some time ago, Lois Kingsley Pelton wrote a poem which is a
vivid description of a lost soul:

Iconoclast

He spurned time's legacy and laughed aloud
At such antiquities as right and wrong
And faith and beauty. These were for the crowd,
Whose brains were simple—he, himself, was strong.
His greatest pleasure was in tearing down
The altars other men had built. He mocked
At everything, and, like a crown
He wore his disbelief. At last, he locked
Himself within an ego-tower, then,
One evening, suddenly, he looked about
And knew he was the loneliest of men.
There was no virtue anywhere to flout,
No image left to break, but only earth,
The stars he could not reach; or death; or birth! [20]

In actual practice then, the counsel of skepticism strikes at
the trust and confidence which underlie and are indispensable to
the growth of personality. It sows the seeds of doubt as to the
reliability, the trustworthiness of men. It puts the self on the defensive, it transforms the expansive view of life into the contractive; it moves the self in the direction of becoming a lost soul. If

the skeptic points out the basis for distrust in life, he should consider Professor Nicolai Hartmann's balancing of that case: "Credulity, too ready trustfulness, is a serious fault . . . but habitual distrust, the opposite fault, is morally far more flagrant, a rooted skepticism in regard to moral character, . . . community, whether national or intimately private, is always a community of faith . . . distrust breaks all bond . . . faith is the capacity for cooperation . . . distrust is impotence . . . faith is the basis which supports everything else." [21]

Skepticism has nothing constructive to offer in the presence of division and discord in life. It can make but cannot heal such breaches in human relationships. To live is to misunderstand, to be misunderstood. Every man both injures others and is injured by them upon occasion. One of the most persistent problems in life is how to deal with this very fact. How to heal the breach? Skepticism asks, "Why bother?" or, "Why think it will be any better if you give him another chance?" It literally has nothing to offer which will lead toward reconciliation.

In the area of larger social relationships, the hand of skepticism continues to be the hand of confusion and disintegration. When it touches a marriage, the home dissolves. Let it enter into a peace conference and the seeds of a new war are sown. Skepticism has nothing constructive to contribute toward the achievement of peace—this fact our so-called realistic generation must master. Mr. Aldous Huxley, who, after a sojourn in the wilderness of skepticism a decade ago, has now developed a vital religious faith, suggests as a first step toward social stability, "If you don't care for men, you can't possibly understand them; all your acuteness will be another form of stupidity." This drives to the heart of much of the present tension in the world between Soviet Russia on the one hand and her erstwhile allies on the other. Mr. John Foster Dulles stands in the forefront of those who are greatly concerned about the proper strategy for coming to a peaceful understanding with Soviet Russia. He is convinced that it can be found and that the way lies in our ability to demonstrate a number of things: "First, that we genuinely cherish for ourselves and others the spiritual and intellectual freedoms which the Soviet system would take away, and that we are willing to sacrifice to preserve them; Second, that those freedoms, which in the past have gloriously served mankind, are still the means whereby men can steadily advance their own development." [22]

There is no work or place in such a program for the skeptic. Only men of great faith in the reality of God and the trustworthiness of men will be able to work with real effectiveness in this undertaking. Skepticism is more than a counsel of despair, it is the counsel of destruction in all great social causes.

To say that skepticism is a lost cause spiritually is but to sum up much that has been said in the preceding pages and to draw certain proper and important religious implications. Measure skepticism by its fruits in human life and affairs, and it is a worse alternative than even the most fanatical sort of religious faith. For while fanaticism will wreck life in a fury of dogmatism, intolerance, or self-righteousness, it at least believes that life is worth wrecking and that there is something even more important than life itself because of which rebels deserve to have their lives wrecked. Skepticism wrecks life too, sometimes swiftly but more often slowly, yet it adds insult to injury by saying that life isn't worth the wrecking.

An inquiry after the enduring contributions of a thoroughgoing skepticism to human life generally yields a most niggardly reward. Grant that a doubting, questioning edge is one essential in the growth of science, philosophy, and religion, and that is about all that can be said. But that lacks a lot of being genuine skepticism since it is coupled with great faith and yields a body of affirmations for thought and life. Skepticism does not do this. When it is in charge of a man's spirit, his interest and energy drop to zero.

IV

A study of the nature of skepticism justifies some sharp conclusions about its usefulness for living. It is the last refuge of the intellectual and ethical sluggard. It offers an escape from the necessity of struggling for long-range ideals by the simple strategy of doubting the reality of the ideals themselves. It offers an escape from the necessity of action under the guidance of conscience and judgment by doubting the reality of conscience and judgment. It is an ominous sign of deep spiritual crisis that men are again lifting the banner of skepticism—a cause that begins by degrading them and ends by betraying them!

It is the high calling of religious faith to declare without ceasing the bankruptcy of skepticism as an adequate creed for living in this or any other day. This must be done not only in words but, even more importantly, in a life of great faith in God and man. These are indescribably difficult and anxious days for men and women who profess the Christian faith. For, in addition to sharing the anxiety characteristic of this tragic hour in history, they feel a crushing responsibility to find some creative way out. The world is openly acknowledging in word and deed the collapse of its faith in itself and is seeking a faith in something other than itself. I cannot recall a more auspicious time for the immediate and incessant proclamation of the essential Christian faith. We must proclaim with every power at our disposal the central fact in life as viewed by the Christian religion. That central fact is the reality of the One Universal God, the Father of us all, most clearly revealed in the life and teachings of Jesus Christ.

When I say "Jesus Christ," I am not using the words in any magical sense. I mean the man who confronted Pilate in that little courtyard in Jerusalem nearly two thousand years ago. You will search the literature of history in vain for a greater contrast between two men. Pilate was motivated by the fear of what the Jews were saying and doing, by the fear of what Caesar might think and do about his decision. Jesus was sustained by faith in God, and by that alone. Gone were the quiet walks through Galilee, the land that he loved. At an end were the long discussions with his disciples about the essentials of their faith. The time for faith incarnate, for *sheer* faith, if you please, was at hand. Thank God he measured up! With greater provocation toward skepticism than most of us will ever have, he continued in the line of faith and confidence in God and man. There is no room for real doubt about the fact that the God of history has rendered a decisive verdict in the age-old yet ever contemporary conflict between men of doubt and men of faith in the living God. It is a fact capable of experimental validation—if we have the courage and the love to try it—that the God of love is a God of strength to one who would be a living witness to Him.

The task of Christians, then, is to present God to themselves and to the world as that Fact and Factor in existence about whose reality there can no longer be any significant dispute. It is the part of reasoned understanding to approach Him as the Judge of all the earth, whose judgments are issued in justice and mercy. It is the part of wisdom to hail Him as the Creator, Sustainer, and Redeemer of life. It is the mark of rational confidence to work with Him as Comrade and call Him Friend in time of trouble, our Strength in crisis. When we feel beaten—as we shall many times—let us take new strength from the vision of "That strange man hanging on the cross." For it is as true now as then: "In Him was life and the life was the light of men."

Chapter III ⋞§§⋟ CAN THE BLIND
LEAD THE BLIND?*

I

Many contemporary intellectuals find themselves in an enervating and altogether hopeless predicament. This is their problem: How guide their lives by personal and social purpose in a world which they feel to be devoid of ultimate meaning? The confused state of their quest for a purpose sufficiently compelling to integrate their loyalties speaks for itself. Some seek to solve the problem by excessive activity within their special fields and are known in the earlier stages as "promising young thinkers" and in the latter stages as "tired young intellectuals." Others lift high the banner of some great social cause and endeavor to rally their confused comrades round it, but they seldom look beyond the cause. All too few realize that one of the perennial functions of the Christian religion has been to rescue intellectuals from precisely this cul-de-sac; that it has the light and leading they so sorely need; that it is languishing for lack of what they have to offer as truly as they languish for lack of what it can contribute.

Quite naturally, the concept "intellectual," reflecting the confusion of the intellectuals, has many meanings in current usage. Jacques Barzun suggests one: "The power to propel a thought even half an inch beyond the vulgar notion is in fact the only thing that divides the intellectual class from the rest." [1] But that smacks of unwarranted snobbery. As I shall be using it, it connotes neither disparagement nor commendation. It is, rather, an

* Much of this chapter appeared in *Religion in Life*, Winter, 1940, under the title "The Intellectuals' Crisis in Religion."

attempt at accurate description. *The intellectual is one who strives to see phenomena in their context.* He believes that the objects of his interest can be understood only when viewed as integral aspects of a larger whole. The nonintellectual, in contrast, is content to take things as they come. He inquires into the whence and whyness of their coming and the whitherness of their going only insofar as such inquiries facilitate immediate adjustment. The intellectual rigorously insists that these are fundamental questions and must be answered up to the limit of our information if even immediate adjustments are to escape the category of guesswork, if not sheer opportunism. One of the major fights of his life is against the sin of oversimplification. In this, he knows, lies the power and the peril of yellow journalism, mob action, the frenzied appeals of demagogues in all walks of life. Consequently he is prepared to oppose it on all fronts even though the charges of "pedantry" and "academic" be heaped upon him by self-styled realists and practical souls.

Aristotle disposes of the nonintellectual in a single, cutting sentence: "He who takes only a few things into account finds it easy to pronounce judgment." Matthew Arnold's celebrated description of Sophocles may well be taken as the end and aim of all intellectual endeavor: "He saw life steadily and saw it whole." When Thomas Aquinas defines God as Perfect Intellect he means simply that God sees the causal strata of creation—past, present, and future—as a vast totality, one unified panorama unfolded before him. This, of course, is Ideal Intellection and, by definition, open only to God, the Omniscient.

Although our entire educational procedure is now under fire, much of it deserved, it has been and continues to be one vast laboratory for the nurture of intellectuals, of persons who are trained to see some phenomena, at least, as aspects of a larger whole. It is only fair to say that the sole reason for the professional existence of universities and libraries and of professors and the books they write is their ability accurately to indicate perspectives on fields of facts. The expert is one who sees the underlying, the more comprehensive, relationships of a special field.

The geologist moves from a stone to a stratum to a formative epoch in the earth's crust. The archaeologist discovers what strikes most of us as a handful of pieces of pottery, but he sees in them the remnants of an urn characteristic of a definite type of culture which he is able to reconstruct on the basis of this and related discoveries. The social scientist begins with an institution, say the family; he considers it from the angle of its development; he contrasts the form which prevails in our culture with that which obtains in others; he considers the disruptive tendencies within the present institutional structure such as divorce rate, later marriage age, and changing moral conventions regarding sex behavior.

And so it goes throughout our educational system. It takes as freshmen persons whose perspective on various phenomena is narrowly limited and plans to graduate those who have known the thrill as well as the chill of retreating horizons. The fundamental aim of education is to emancipate us from the atomicity of sensation. This it does by teaching us to seek the meaning of the things we experience, believe, and strive for in their broadest context. More and more the leaders in the field of education are coming to agreement on the point that, if education is to escape the provincialism of specialization, it must result in a world view, a conception of the total life enterprise. The Harvard report on *General Education in a Free Society* [2] puts it succinctly: "Taken as a whole, education seeks to do two things: help young persons fulfill the unique, particular functions in life which it is in them to fulfill, and fit them so far as it can for those common spheres which, as citizens and heirs of a joint culture, they will share with others." That education has not done this satisfactorily is the premise of the report, and it seeks to bring to the surface the reasons for the failure and the changes that must be made if success is to be achieved. Chancellor Robert Hutchins has gone so far as to insist that metaphysics should be considered the basic discipline in college work.

Needless to say, education so conceived is immediately beset by the peril of accepting some one world view as final and devoting its energies to securing acceptance of this viewpoint. An apologist is notoriously deficient in self-criticism. An educational system that is long on exposition and evangelism is bound to be short on comprehension and criticism. The school systems of totalitarian regimes are a case in point. They teach a world view, one dictated by political or economic or national considerations. History and science are rewritten, not to mention falsified, in order to bolster that world view. Consequently, the products of these schools are not so much intellectuals as addicts.

We who are interested in religion heavily underscore the notion that the intellectual has fallen short of his logical development unless he finally arrives at a world view. But we are suspicious of any known world view so rigidly complete that it tries to give the lie to the value and validity of growth through experience. In other words we feel, to adopt the thought of the Pilgrim pastor, that "new light" is always breaking forth in the area of human experience. We must keep on insisting that every world view must have a growing edge, that it should not be placed above and beyond the criticisms of cumulative experience and reflection. Therefore, we must insist that the quest of the intellectual is not and cannot be considered complete until and unless he has come to terms with the place and meaning of religion in his world view. This is precisely what most intellectuals have not done. We can safely say that the most far-reaching crisis confronting them today springs from their indecision and ignorance regarding religion. We are beginning to realize that there is something fundamentally dangerous rather than merely naïve about a man who, while an expert in economics, let us say, muddles along with no religion or with scant regard for it, or with a ten-year-old conception of it. Yet that is precisely the situation in which our intellectuals find themselves today.

II

Some intellectuals regard religion as dangerous and worthy of extermination both because it is surcharged with superstition and because it impedes social change. Religion has been guilty of these crimes at certain times in history, but that it has always played and must necessarily play this role is manifestly false to anyone who studies with care any one of half a dozen different historical epochs in the last three millenniums.

Other intellectuals, like George Santayana, regard religion as a form of poignant art and feel that as such it deserves its board and keep. But this limited view of the scope of religion can be maintained only by the indefensible procedure of overlooking or minimizing those creative ethical insights of religion which at different crucial periods have rocked empires and refashioned social structure in general. I refer to (1) the prophetic reforms in Judah in the seventh century B.C.; (2) the alterations within the Roman Empire due to the impact of Christianity; (3) the sweeping Cluniac reforms in the direction of checking the ravages of feudal warfare in the early eleventh century; (4) the Lollard movement in England in the fourteenth century, which was a vital feeder to the sixteenth-century English Reformation; (5) the Wesleyan movement in England in the eighteenth century with its profound social reverberations.

And then there are other intellectuals like T. S. Eliot, Christopher Dawson, and Rosalind Murray, who accept some specific form of religion as the *true interpretation* and use it as the basis for reinterpreting life as a spiritual enterprise. They seek the altar of religion so conceived and consecrate their critical abilities, historical insights, and social passion to its service.

Thus we see trained minds in the arts, sciences, and philosophy ignoring, rejecting, tolerating, and embracing religion. And it is both because there is no other conceivable alternative and because intellectuals find themselves willy-nilly choosing one or the other of these that they must rethink the problem of their relationship to religion.

Yet it is not hard to understand why the intellectual, trained as he is in either art, science, or philosophy, moves cautiously when he approaches religion. For religion has had several pitched battles with all three disciplines within the last five hundred years.

These major periods of conflict continue to loom large in modern culture: the Renaissance, when religion, proud mistress of the minds and souls of men for fourteen centuries, found herself challenged by a revolt of the entire range of the arts; the Enlightenment, when philosophy, emboldened by the rich fruition of minds like Bacon, Descartes, Hume, Kant, and others, drew up and made good her declaration of independence from religion; the nineteenth century, when scientific method laid "profane" hands on the problems of the origin and nature of man, a province hitherto gladly left to religion. In none of these ages did religion quietly abdicate. Led by doughty warriors whose zeal for the faith of their fathers far outstripped their appreciative insight into the values of the opposition, she plunged into the fray. Not only were the torments of hell paraded before the eyes of the unbelievers, but in an appalling number of cases generous samples of what it would be like were served up here on earth. It is a long, dark, sickening story and illustrates why intellectuals are wary of religion.

Nevertheless, intellectuals, individually and collectively, can be rescued from aimlessness only by getting a firm grasp on two emphases that are fundamentally religious in nature; (1) Human values are neither optional nor arbitrary but are organic to the universe. (2) The achievement of these values is a social process. When I say the intellectual needs these religious affirmations, I am, of course, assuming that when he surveys the human scene, he is moved to do something about the problems which harass men. If he can survey the agony and unrest of our day with the detachment that enabled Goethe to watch Napoleon storm and sack a city and only marvel at the manifestation of sheer force exhibited, then the intellectual has a very limited and definitely irreligious perspective on the life enterprise. It is wholly beside my present point to try to convince intellectuals that they ought to do something about the problems which agitate men. My belief in their integrity compels me to assume, in the first place, that they see at least some of these problems, in the second place, that they want to do something about them, and in the third place, that they are wondering what religion has to offer under the circumstances.

The first thing it offers is the insistence that the human values indicated by the great class concepts, truth, beauty, goodness, and love, some or all of which the intellectual may respect, are not simply human constructions but indicate certain actual and possible relationships between man and the rest of nature. Life as it expresses itself in and through man is a definite yet dynamic thing. It streams into the future, yet does not lose its identity. Its genius is its forward thrust along lines determined both by its own nature and by what the environment permits. It is a half-truth to say, as religious humanism does, that life is a bundle of desires, the other half being that these desires depend for their fulfillment upon the nature of both the human organism and the environment. We desire food, yet the desire per se is no guarantee that food will be forthcoming, nor is it any assurance that what we call food will be healthful. Most of us will unhesitatingly affirm that health is a human value, yet it is far from a purely human construction. It is in reality a very complex pattern of interrelationships between man and his world, involving breathing, eating, drinking, sleeping, playing, working, and many complicated physiological processes. While we may define health any way we please, we cannot be healthy by doing anything we choose, *unless we choose wisely*. Life speaks the final word on all our definitions.

All of which is fairly obvious in the realm of health, yet the fundamental principle involved in it applies to the great values mentioned earlier: truth, beauty, goodness, and love. They are human reactions insofar as they represent our groping efforts to discover and clarify the meaning of life, actual and potential. Yet they do not stream forth from human life like a flag from a flagpole, unattached at the far end. Rather they are attempts to describe a relationship which does exist in some measure and may through wise choices and purposive living exist in greater measure. Wherever and whenever you find life, regardless of form or level of existence, you find adaptations designed to sustain and promote the continuity of the structure. Though life on the human level is so complex that we, with all of our science, have only begun to explore its mysteries, it manifests that same primal urge to sustain and promote itself by adjustments to the total environment. Truth, beauty, goodness, and love are ways of describing certain types of adjustment, certain modes of relationship, which we have discovered in part, and which invite further exploration and experimentation.

And there are other concepts, opposites of the ones just mentioned: deception, ugliness, meanness, and hatred. These likewise connote certain relationships which man can and does sustain to the world. And the difference between the two sets of relationships is determined by what happens to life when it is enmeshed in them. The relationships gathered into the categories of truth, beauty, goodness, and love progressively enrich life; they move in the direction of the more abundant life—one in which the capacities of men are discovered, nurtured, and brought to rich fruition; one characterized by health rather than sickness, wisdom rather than ignorance, brotherliness rather than condescension, understanding rather than prejudice. Conversely, the relationships which are instances of deception, ugliness, meanness, and hatred progressively strip life of meaning and worth and finally destroy the very thing they feed on.

The Christian religion centers attention upon the value structure of the universe, calling it God, and insists that the abundant life flows from one type of interaction with this rather than another. To the doubter it can only say: try and see. If you can be healthy without conforming, consciously or not, to the laws of well-being which are implicit in our personalities; if you can enjoy deep friendships without conforming, consciously or not, to the laws governing personal association which, though we know them only in part, are implicit in our structure; if you can create the Great Society, that social structure which seeks to discover, nurture and bring to rich fulfillment the creative energies of man, without paying strict and humble attention to the laws of personal and social growth which are implicit in human beings and societies—in short, if you can succeed in living a full and abundant life governed by the hypothesis that

"I am the master of my fate
I am the captain of my soul,"

then religion has nothing more to say. Religion has never paid much attention to verbal atheism—to the man who says there is no God; but it has always been profoundly stirred by ethical atheism—by the man who acts as though there were no God. It has consistently submitted its fundamental conviction that there is a value structure implicit in nature to the test of action, of life. "By their fruits shall ye know them."

III

Religion offers the intellectual a way, and the only way, out of the bewilderment and cynicism which so easily beset him by confronting him with a categorical imperative in the form of *a consciousness of work to be done*. It is idle to talk about "purposive living" apart from a sense of *oughtness*, a conviction of purpose in life, which is its very foundation. Something worth living for, something worth committing oneself to, body, mind, and soul, something worth dying for swims into the ken of the intellectual when he couples with his vision of work to be done the profoundly rational and mystical consciousness that the reason it ought to be done derives from the very structure of the universe as it comes to expression in human life. He will appropriate as food for his spirit Dean Inge's trenchant insight that "Homage to the ultimate values is the worship of God."

This, then, is the first and the great contribution of religion to the intellectual: His purposes and the purpose of God can coincide, for, as Whitehead reminds us, "The Purpose of God is the achievement of Value in the temporal world." The second contribution is closely related to the first, and can be stated this way: The achievement of human values is a social process.

The Christian religion is not only prepared to recognize the

point now agreed upon by social psychologists, that we are children of nature and that our self is a social creation, but it pushes
on to make that most profound of all affirmations of our social
nature, namely, that we are sons of God and brothers one of
another. It draws a single staggering ethical corollary from this
affirmation: the only way to approach God is by serving, through
love, our fellow men. Ethical religion, then, is a call to action,
social action, in terms of problems, social problems, in the name
and for the sake of God, the value structure of the universe. "No
one observatory is equal to the tasks of astronomy," says a famous astronomer. Neither is any one man, or group of men, or
culture equal to the task of discovering the fuller meaning of
truth, beauty, goodness, and love in terms of the problems of our
day. This is a shared undertaking, broad enough to include and
profit by the contributions of all sincere and intelligent men
everywhere. It lays every sensitive spirit and discerning mind
under obligation to share the best that he has without thought or
restraint or reward and to continually refine what he thinks best
in the fires of life. If these great values are to be anything more
than ivory towers in which we hide while storms engulf the
world of men, then all who are in search of them must join hands.

One of the noblest instances of goodness of which Chicago
boasts is Hull House. Although we always, and rightly, think of
Jane Addams when we think of Hull House, it far transcends the
work of any one person's hands. One of Jane Addams' outstanding gifts was her ability as a social engineer; for she channeled
into her project the hope, aspirations, and aid of unnumbered
thousands of others. Hull House is what it is today because it is
the product of the shared efforts of all these folk. Without some
such institution those hopes, aspirations, and efforts which have
gone into its effectiveness would have been ephemeral, inchoate,
useless. When gasoline explodes in a chamber created to conserve
its power, appropriate action results. If it explodes anywhere else,
a flash, heat, and smoke occur, and it all adds up to either destruction or uselessness.

The great religions of the world are great precisely because they have mastered this principle of the production and direction of human energies. Without exception they have created a "body of believers," a church, which not only strives to evoke mystic rapport with God and make a rational statement of its faith but, in addition, turns the energies thus generated toward the solution of social problems. Such an organization molds the believers into a mystic whole which is pre-eminently practical in that the unique contribution of each believer is integrated in and directed by common loyalties and goals. The organization trains its leaders and educates its members in the faith, and constantly reconsecrates itself to the cause it serves.

The Christian church with all its faults, and they are many and grievous, is the social institution in our culture which is dedicated to the task of making the ethical insights of the Christian religion socially effective. Many intellectuals feel that the church is so immersed in traditionalism, so entangled with the *status quo*, that it cannot speak an effective word toward social reform. Believing this, they must then choose either to forsake the ethical meaning of religion and attempt to confine it to a way of thinking and a mode of feeling, or to attempt the incredibly difficult task of founding a new social organization capable of conveying the ethical implications of religion to society. This latter alternative is acceptable if, and only if, the church of our day is beyond redemption.

While Jack London would not rank high among the intellectual leaders of his generation, he was considerably more than an adventure-story writer. He was a thoughtful student of society and an avowed socialist. He sought to propel his thoughts "half an inch beyond the vulgar notion. . . ." He and most of his friends rejected the church. Shortly before his death in 1916 one of his friends wrote urging him to join in a concerted attack on religion. Jack London replied, "The battle over religion seems so far away, a little and forgotten battle still being waged off somewhere in a secret corner of the earth. I think you are fighting an antagonist already, intellectually, beaten." These words furnish strange reading today, scarcely a quarter of a century after they were penned. We know now that Jack London was quite wrong in his prophecy. The spiritual resources of religion have never been more squarely in the limelight of human life and history than they are today. But it is not enough simply to record the fact that Jack London was wrong. What we need to know is this: Why did he—intelligent, earnest social reformer that he was —think that religion was on its way out? Why is it that so many of his as well as our own contemporaries shared and share that opinion? What lies back of their judgment on religion?

It is not difficult to reconstruct London's line of reasoning. It runs something like this: Religion is now thousands of years old; it has had the longest try at meeting human needs of any existing social institution. The record is now clear—religion has failed to make good its claim to help mankind toward the more abundant life. The biggest reason back of this failure is that religion is afraid of social reform because it is wedded to the *status quo*, which opposes reform. Hence religion has given up the fight to help the common man better his lot through fear of losing the support of the privileged few. Sensing this, the common man is turning away from religion and is now looking to other social forces for help. This, of course, means that the *status quo* is doomed to perish in the vast cataclysm which these social forces will produce when they collide with or erupt within the *status quo*. The laboring man, the farmer, the proletariat, broadly conceived, will take over the reins of power and remake the whole life of mankind. The institutions that are inseparably connected with the *status quo* are doomed; kings and priests, palaces and churches—all are doomed. Believing this to be the trend of events, and believing that religion not only was caught in it but also was unaware of it, Jack London reached the conclusion that religion is "already intellectually beaten." There is nothing especially vindictive toward religion about this judgment. He said the same about the form of government called monarchy and the form of society called capitalism.

But even as London wrote his prophecy of doom, the evidence that religion was not intellectually beaten was beginning to roll in like a tidal wave. Exactly twenty-five years earlier Pope Leo XIII issued his famous encyclical entitled *Rerum Novarum*. Nine years before London counted religion out, Walter Rauschenbusch wrote his *Christianity and the Social Crisis*. Both of these must be regarded as great documents in the evolution of the social conscience of the Christian churches. They are careful statements on the work of the church in an age of social conflict. Their writers, like London and his cohorts, foresaw the character of the tragedy which was to overtake mankind. Standing squarely within the tradition of historical Christianity and both drawing their inspiration and documenting their conclusions from it, they spoke out incisively, courageously, and radically in the name of the churches. What they wrote adds up to several conclusions held in common: (1) Industry must respect in every laborer his dignity as a man and as a child of God; furthermore, this respect must be shown in concrete terms of working conditions, wages, and the right of representation in all matters relating to his livelihood. (2) The church is the messenger of God, not of man or of any given social order; it speaks always in terms of the Kingdom of God. (3) The church is the champion of the poor, the needy, the downtrodden as was its Master. (4) The supreme concern of the Church must be its devotion to caring for these neglected ones in God's family.

It is impossible to exaggerate the influences which these and similar declarations had upon the mind, conscience, and program of the Christian churches of America. Soon every major church group issued *a social creed* embodying these ideas in some form. They began to find steady expression in and through the literature used in the church schools, the Christian Endeavors, and Epworth Leagues of the land. Seminaries and divinity schools began to develop their departments of Christian ethics, paying special attention to contemporary economic and social problems. Aspirants for the ministry were familiarized with the issues underlying industrial strife and were taught to look at them from the vantage point of the towering Christian ideals.

Of course, the occupants of positions of privilege were outraged. They demanded that the church mind its own business and "stick to the gospel." Courageous church leaders like Peabody, Rauschenbusch, Mathews, and Holt replied that, at long last, the church is minding its own business; that wherever the bodies and spirits of men are bowed and broken by problems, there the Christian church has a mission, there the Christian gospel is really a gospel, *good news.*

All this had gathered tremendous headway by the time Jack London counted religion out. Why did he not see it? Two reasons probably account for it. First, the movement was *inside* the church, and he was *outside.* One had to be a sincere and sensitive member of the church to understand the profound changes that were coming into being. Then, too, for London the barricade loomed so large as the only way to secure social reform that it never occurred to him that any good could be won by the less spectacular, more natural means of development.

Our contemporary Jack Londons, publicly prophesying or quietly anticipating the crack-up of religion, ought to profit by London's error and acquaint themselves with "the deep things of God" that are happening within the Christian churches today. They ought to know that some of the severest critics of the *status quo* at those points where it neglects or distorts human rights draw their nourishment from Christian principles. It is easy, I know, to be complacent about the pronouncements of church conferences. But it is a dangerous error either to ignore them or to underestimate them as so many of us do. They are drawn up and passed, in most cases, by bodies composed of laity and clergy alike who are determined to relate the eternal principles of the Christian faith to the problems that are crucifying civilization today. Their conclusions have been anything but comforting. Recent church conferences in England and America have startled conservatives and sobered radicals. And the end is not yet! They, and other gatherings like them, are indications that the problems of social reform are going to occupy the minds of serious churchmen from now on. Whoever seeks out the church today or tomorrow as a place where he can quiet his rising blood pressure over social reform is certain to be a misinformed and unhappy individual. We begin with the recognition of the plain fact that this is not a Christian civilization. It is lunacy to assert that any social order based upon, proceeding by, and pointing inevitably into one ruinous war after another is even remotely acquainted with the basic ideals of Christian ethics. To say this, we know, is as truly an indictment of the Christian church as it is of any other institution in our social order, for the church is the oldest of them all and presumably must admit the truth of the charge that she has been lying down on her job. But to confess this as a sin is the point at which we begin our contemporary Christian approach to the world crisis.

Jack London and his contemporary colleagues make two basic mistakes when they prophesy the doom of religion. In the first place, they usually operate on some sort of mechanistic theory of the universe. For them, we live in a universe of laws without purpose, matter without mind, and body without spirit. Now Christian thinkers are acutely aware of the reality of laws, matter, and body, but they insist that purpose, mind, and spirit are equally real. They know that the claim alone does not solve the problem of how laws and purpose, matter and mind, body and spirit actually do go together. But they believe that somehow they do belong together since we never find them separately. Insofar as this is true, any mechanistic theory of reality is ruled out as inadequate, and all attempts to demonstrate the law of the economic determination of history, for example, are foredoomed to failure.

The second error the skeptical Londons fall prey to is this: they have an amazingly superficial acquaintance with the explosive character of religion. It is always deeper than any race or church or social instrument through which it may work. It is always bursting out in new forms and directions at the most unexpected times and places. A close study of Christian history prepares one to expect the unexpected! When all about it men are losing faith and courage, religion begins to sing its songs of hope and confidence. Only the Exile could have produced Second Isaiah with his exquisite, probing "Songs of the Suffering Servant." Confronted by this paradox, you wonder why and by what right religion reacts in this fashion. Is it not something like whistling in the dark? Not at all! Religion begins to take God seriously when every other prop is knocked out from under it. When we see our most careful plans end up in chaos, our fondest hopes laid waste, and our cherished institutions battered to pieces, then we have nothing left but God to rely on. Then we begin to believe in God as a holy Fact and Factor in human life.

IV

Before relegating the church to the museum the intellectual should spend some time studying the present state of the church and avoid the error of Jack London. When this is done he will see two facts: (1) More water has gone under the bridge of religion in the last twenty-five years than in any other quarter-century since the Reformation; the entire church structure, ecclesiastical, theological, and ethical, is in a condition of rapid and epoch-making change. (2) The church, with its profound prophetic tradition, is the only institution protesting and capable of endless resistance against the exploitation of human values by social and political organizations for narrow and vicious ends.

Apropos of the first fact, mention should be made of Charles Beard's survey of significant trends in American life and institutions in the last two decades, *America in Midpassage*, which simply omits the church. Nowhere is mention made of the developments in church policies and politics that have been going on with increasing speed for the last half-century. Dr. Beard, like other intellectuals, either does not know or has made no attempt to evaluate the far-reaching implications of a multitude of movements, for example: (1) the growth in importance of the Federal Council of the Protestant Churches of Christ in America, and of the World Council of Churches; (2) the rapidly rising educational standards for the clergy; (3) the organization of committees on social problems, councils for social action, federations for social service, and similar organs for keeping the churches alert on social issues; (4) the rapid spread of religious work on college

and university campuses; (5) the increasing amount of co-operation among religious groups, epitomized by the National Conference of Christians and Jews. How far these and related
movements will go depends, of course, not alone on the quality of
clergymen but even more definitely on the quality of the laymen
who will rally to their support in a realistic manner.

Nor can intellectuals blindly ignore the plain truth of the second fact: the Christian churches have been one of the strongest
bulwarks against the ready realization of the totalitarian goals set
by various governments. We should not claim too much for the
churches in this matter but neither should we claim too little.
Long after the labor organizations, dissenting political factions,
and the educational system had been "co-ordinated" by the Nazi
government the "church problem" remained *and remained to the
end* as one of the great unsolved internal problems of that state.
This simple fact, which occasions no surprise in one acquainted
with Christian history, confronts the intellectual with a challenge
that he cannot ignore with good conscience.

Then, too, the churches are producing some of the most incisive critics of contemporary trends in civilization. The Oxford
Conference studies [3] are as valuable a critique of the modern
world as can be found. They dispose of the notion that the church
is helplessly entangled in the *status quo*. They also demonstrate
the reality and value of the religious perspective on human events
and problems. The differences of opinion which they contain are
expressions of vitality and growth rather than disintegration since
they are contributions toward the achievement of a deeper unity
among divergent movements in Christianity.

The realistic way the World Council of Churches went about
the task of bracing the churches for the shock of the war and is
now leading them into the tasks of peace must commend itself to
thoughtful persons as one of the significant advances of the last
twenty-five years. The firm reaction of the churches to the restoration of the legal basis of the liquor business is that of an institution which senses its mission and is prepared to carry it out
by educational, legal, and spiritual means. The increasing facilities
for bringing the influence of the churches to bear upon policies

in economics and politics alike bespeak a vigilance that will prove valuable.

The point I am trying to make is that the church is not only in existence but also in motion. I do not see how the intellectuals can long ignore these facts if they are actually in earnest in their determination both to understand more fully and to influence more deeply the swift-moving events of today. They are right in being critical of religion, in demanding to know whether it is living or dead. For there are certain well-defined situations in which religion finds itself intellectually beaten and the discerning thinker wants to know whether or to what extent contemporary religion is in any of them.

Religion, both personal and social, is intellectually beaten when it finds itself in any one of three situations: The first is when it is unable to state its beliefs with cogency and conviction. For the essence of religion is beliefs that are profoundly believed. It must be able to make a forthright appeal to the mind, to reason, to logical order and system. It must be able to ask and answer questions, to relate itself to the problems and facts of the human enterprise. For religion to ask a man to believe something he does not understand is a studied insult to his humanity. But challenging him to achieve a clear and cogent system of beliefs is to pay tribute to that "spark of divinity" which all men have or are. Vital religion, then, must be able and will be gladly willing to state, clarify, and defend its views or philosophy of life. It will leap at every chance to give a reason for the hope that is within it. This forever removes it from reliance upon hearsay evidence, however hallowed it may be by some great tradition. It is, I take it, no accident that the history of Christian polemics is in reality a history of the great controversies in and through which the Christian faith grew to intellectual maturity. In this ability to meet internal and external criticism and challenge lies the secret of its tremendous triumphs where other religions have failed. The only generalization as to growth permitted by Christian history is that ancient watchword: "Ye shall know the truth and the truth shall make you free."

A second situation in which religion is intellectually beaten is when it is unable to revise the meaning of its inherited symbols or to develop new ones to replace them. By symbols I mean such things as the Bible, communion or the Lord's Supper, baptism, and the church. To say that they are symbols is to say that they are centers of meaning which far transcend their physical reality. The Bible is worlds more than a book with a certain number of pages. The elements used in the Lord's Supper, taken by themselves, constitute the slenderest of fare, but seen at the center of the meanings which they elicit they are "food for the full-grown." What has happened to cause these hallowed symbols to become "strayed ghosts of an earlier age" to so many of our generation? Dr. Alfred North Whitehead suggests a possible answer that ought to shake us out of sentimental repose: "Those societies which cannot combine reverence for their symbols with freedom of revision must ultimately decay either from anarchy or from the slow atrophy of a life stifled by useless shadows."

Consider for a moment what this means when applied to the Bible, for example. At one time the Bible was the symbol of infallible truth to most Protestant Christians. But that was half a century or more ago! Now the most that a thoughtful student can claim for it is that it contains the deepest insights we have into man's search for God and God's response to man. But it is far from infallible. Many Christians over the last two generations have cast a skeptical eye on this change in meaning. They said: "It's all or nothing for me! If I can't believe all the Bible I'll believe none of it!" Of course this all-or-nothing dilemma usually wound up at *nothing*, if not for the fathers, then for their children. The upshot of it all is that we have a biblically illiterate generation of otherwise fairly well-informed persons on our hands. And we in churches have our own woodenheaded way of handling the Bible to thank for it, too! Having admitted that, we must now lay plans for capturing and recapturing the loyalty and interest of practically an entire generation of young men and women. If we cannot do that, we as churchmen must own up to it that we are intellectually beaten.

The third situation in which religion sustains intellectual defeat is when it is unable to grapple with the problems which harass its devotees. There is no such thing as a good religion that isn't good for something in terms of daily difficulties. Out of its rich fund of human experience, religion can frequently furnish concrete answers and recommendations, though it has no catalogue of blueprints guaranteed to cover every situation. But where it cannot provide the answers it can provide courage, hope, and faith sufficient to sustain us as we hammer out the answers; it can provide a fellowship of like-minded persons upon whom we can rely for encouragement and support; it can throw open the possibility of achieving a faith in the reality of a God whose nature it is to be righteous and merciful.

The central symbol of the Christian religion—the Cross—has been, from the beginning, a token of the fact that God Himself is seeking to solve the tragedy of human life. When our fathers invited men to take up the Cross of Christ they were issuing an invitation to join God in this cosmic undertaking. That was and is a searching invitation *and it still holds good* wherever the Christian religion, conscious of its mission, confronts men conscious of the human tragedy.

It follows, then, that an intellectually victorious religion is neither an inheritance nor an accident. A clear-cut personal faith requires as much time and attention as a firm grasp on one's profession. And it will be the breath of life to his profession! A vigorous institutional religion requires the consistent and conscientious support of a large number of alert men and women. There is a place and need in religion for every person. One of the strongest guarantees we have of winning the world we need is to find our place in that fellowship and carry our share of its load.

V

I have tried not to give the impression that the intellectuals are simply to be on the receiving end of religion. That would be untrue. Organized religion needs the intellectuals as badly as they needs its affirmations and its fellowship. It needs their information, their ability to approach with disciplined method and thought those areas which they have studied and are studying; it needs the tremendous potency of life—past, present, and future—which, in measure, throbs through their training and personalities. They can bring objectivity and information about concrete problems into the area of religion, and these alone can beat down some of our inherited superstitions and prejudices. Religion in turn can bring confidence, conviction, and humility into their life, giving them the challenge of worship and the comradeship of purposive living.

The intellectuals' crisis in religion, then, is brought on by the fact that they must choose between these alternatives: either reject religion and wander about in a world where values are optional or arbitrary and where nothing really matters—where, as one who chose this course said, "After all, life's quite pointless, isn't it?"; or accept the insight of religion as to the cosmic nature of values and the social nature of their realization and throw their total energies into the church, reforming and energizing it, enabling it to regain a position of vital leadership in the creation of that society which will yet come into existence on this our earth, providing always that we have courage and humility enough to yield to the formative purpose of God. The God of history says to them, as to men of old, "Choose ye this day!"

I

Not long ago we had news of a revolutionary development that promises to help students in the science of astronomy solve one of their most persistent problems. They have known for a long time now that many of the most brilliant stars in the heavens are brilliant not because they are larger than other stars but because they are nearer. Some of the biggest stars show up quite dimly on photographic plates both because they are so far away and because of the brightness of the nearer stars. The recent development is to put a certain kind of film or screen on the lens through which the pictures are made. This screen reduces the light from the nearer and brighter, yet actually smaller, stars, thus enabling astronomers to get a clearer picture of the place and composition of the more distant and dimmer, yet actually larger, ones. It is a first-class triumph in the development of a proper perspective in astronomy.

Offhand I cannot think of anything that is more sadly needed than the extension and application of that principle to human life in general. We are living at a time when, as a character in a recent play put it, ". . . the truest voices are struck down by the loudest." [1] Nearer and smaller concerns crowd more distant and greater ones out of perspective. We find ourselves giving closest attention to whatever or whoever is raising the greatest clamor nearest to us.

How to get and how to keep a proper perspective on things and events is one of the most persistent needs of the day. If there is any one individual who is poorly equipped for living in this particular age, it is the person who "can't see beyond the end of his nose"; one whose imagination and understanding are so warped that he is able to say, "out of sight out of mind."

Yet a selfish and essentially ruthless individualism is sitting on the doorstep of the lives of the best of us all the time. How to keep it from moving in and taking charge of everything until our entire thought and life gravitate around our own personal convenience and comfort is a permanent problem. And not of the individual alone, but of churches, homes, schools, races, and nations! How to get and how to keep a proper perspective on events is the unending quest of the balanced mind and the good life, of the just and good society.

Certainly the Christian churches need to keep everlastingly at the task of achieving such a perspective on events both inside and outside the church. This is easier said than done in the face of every encouragement to ignore or neglect it. We find it easy to become so absorbed in the needs of our local church that we pay scant attention to the greater needs of the Council of Churches in our city, and the still greater needs of the Federal Council of Churches in America, and the still greater needs of the World Council of Churches. Dr. Walter van Kirk in his book, *A Christian Global Strategy*, proves this point beyond all doubt. In 1938 there were approximately twenty-five million adult members in the Protestant churches of the United States. During that year we spent some two hundred seventy-four millions of dollars on our local congregational programs—an average of eleven dollars per person—and an average of about two cents per person for the evangelization of all the non-Christian peoples in the Far East. Dr. van Kirk asks and, in the asking, answers the question, "Does anybody suppose that the world can be conquered for Christ on this basis?" [2]

Yet if the Christian faith is to become an increasingly effective factor in world problems, local churches must win a new and fairer perspective on the relative importance of the work near at hand and that farther away. They must find a way of dimming down the nearer and smaller task in order correctly to appraise the larger and more distant ones. In no other way will they be able to awaken in their members the consciousness of belonging to and sharing in the work of a world-wide communion.

As citizens of this country and of the world community, the need to get and keep a proper perspective on events comes close to being paramount. Simply to state this fact is to underscore its importance. In the long, bloody trek from the simple family group of the cave dweller to a world community man is picking his way through the last and, by all odds, the most dangerous mile of his journey. It is so dangerous in fact that some hysterical voices are urging us to turn back, to try to find a place to live in yesterday's world—the world of sovereign and independent nations. It takes only a moment's reflection to make plain to even the most fearful among us that that way lies only misery, agony, and finally death for everyone.

For nineteen hundred years Christians have been saying that "religion is a way of meeting human needs, of solving the great problems of life." Now an anxious world has a right to ask whether and how religion proposes to help with this matter of reaching a proper perspective on events. Can religion actually tone down the nearer and lesser issues and brighten up the bigger and more distant ones? The answer, without hesitation and with utter conviction is, "Yes!" Vital religion has done this for others; it can do it for us. Vital religion has learned through human experience that it is possible to get and keep life in the proper perspective. This is the special work of the Christian church these days. Not that she has always so considered it! Not that she has ever done it perfectly! But, simply, the prime vocation of the church is to help people put first things first, to bring a standard into life to which "the wise and the just shall repair," to point the way to the abundant life for persons and peoples alike.

Ezekiel's conception of the special vocation of the prophet suggests the special task of the church today. Ezekiel heard the call of God to stand guard over the life of His people. He regarded himself as a divinely appointed watchman over the life and destiny of Israel. He mounted the walls that separated Jerusalem from the rest of the world and divided his time about evenly between looking both ways—inside as well as outside the walls! His divinely imposed duty, he thought, was to warn evildoers to turn to good and doers of good to refrain from evil; to warn the nation when it was moving in the wrong direction and to strengthen it in the right direction. But Ezekiel the prophet was also Ezekiel the Hebrew. He was both part of yet separated from the life of his people. Every anxiety or tragedy that touched them touched him—he was bone of their bone and flesh of their flesh, yet never wholly so. There was always this enormous difference: God had set him apart as His messenger, His prophet, His living voice to Israel. However much an Israelite Ezekiel might be in emotion and desire, his head, will, conscience, and tongue belonged to God and tried to be obedient to Him alone.

We will not be lulled into complacency or led into premature praise of the church if we liken it to a divinely appointed watchman. To cast the church in this role in a realistic manner requires that we reopen the whole matter of what the church actually is, and what it is trying to do. Needless to say, we shall be rowing in deep and stormy waters. We shall be studying a two-thousand-year-old institution and asking how and why it grew from what it was to what it is. We shall be looking at some four hundred different Christian churches and asking, "Does anything bind them together? If so, what is it?"

II

I could almost wish that this question, "What is the Christian church?" were somewhat less pressing than it is today. It would be easier to be dispassionate about it if so much did not hinge upon getting the right answer. But, so far from being academic, it is one of the undodgeable and desperately crucial problems of our time. Our secular, pagan age is learning to its amazement, if not outright chagrin, that the church is not and never has been on trial for the right to be considered a vital, basic fact in human life and history. The ones who have been and are actually on trial today are those who think it does not much matter whether the church lives or dies, who pride themselves on being "objective" about the church, when what they mean is that they think they can get along without it and what it stands for in human life and history.

It is a sobering fact that at least half of the adult citizens of this country take this position. For that is the percentage that are not related to any religious organization in even a tenuous way. Why so many are in this category cannot be explained by any one reason, nor, for that matter, does any list of reasons seem wholly adequate. Undoubtedly, some non-churchmen would agree with Tolstoy, "The church, by transmitting the truth of the doctrine of Jesus, has communicated life to the world. Upon this nourishment the world has grown and developed. But the church has had its day and is now superfluous." [3] Many more would agree with a friend of mine who said, "Well, the church is all right for those who like that sort of thing. But, personally, I don't need it." Still others are undoubtedly alienated from the church by some defect or other in the life and management of the church in general or of a particular church in their community. For one reason or another, or for no clear reason at all, one-half of the citizens of the United States stand entirely outside the life and program of the Christian church. But non-churchmen are not willing to face the fact that it is they and not the church who are on trial in these days when creative undertakings and institutions are struggling for survival.

In the face of this situation, we will not want to spend time fondling comforting but ambiguous statements about the nature and the purpose of the Christian Church. Yet it is not easy to get a clear and compelling answer to the question, "What is the church?" The Oxford Conference (1937) spent many hours wrestling with it, and the Oxford Conference books [4] kept referring to it as the crucial question before the Christian church today. We could use the Pauline figure and liken the church to "the body of Christ," [5] or the familiar creedal formula, "one catholic and apostolic church." Such descriptions are richly endowed with tradition as well as concrete meanings. But they are also theological battlegrounds over which men have fought for several hundred years. And we have had enough of such wars, if there is any way to avoid them. It is possible that, by trying a new approach, we shall be able to circumvent some of these theological controversies. Like Edmund Gosse, I prefer, wherever possible, "to let sleeping dogmas lie."

The simplest, most direct answer to the question, "What is the church?" is this: "It is a religious communion." That yields a clue to its nature and sketches its purpose in a sentence.

To say that the church is a communion distinguishes it at once from any other institution. For the center of the church is not a particular kind of organization, or a special set of sacraments, or a creed, or a liturgy, or even the Bible—important as all these are in the total life of the church. The church, essentially, is an assembly of people in rapt adoration of a vision: "And we beheld His glory as the only begotten Son of God." The church is the disciples listening to the Sermon on the Mount and beholding heaven and earth fused together in the holy will of God. The church is the disciples rushing to the empty tomb, or gathered in the upper room waiting, waiting, waiting. The church is Peter eying the leaders of Judaism and saying, "We must obey God rather than men!" Wherever men's lives are made luminous by the light of God as seen in Jesus Christ, there is the church.

For this vision both created the church in New Testament times and sustained it through the recurring persecutions of the latter days of the Roman Empire. It has kept the church going and growing through the centuries. The church is an institution, to be sure, but it is an institution growing out of the vision of God in Christ. And that endows it with some striking characteristics which have been recognized by Christians from the very beginning of the church's historic career. It is "in but not of the world." It is "a separate people"; a people "set apart by God"; a people "commissioned by God." It was no light matter to step into that early fellowship. The ones who did so were asked to re-examine all normal associations, interests, and possessions in the light of the new vision. They were asked to recenter their life in its meaning. As a result, they became "new creatures in Christ." After centuries of making participation in the church easier and easier, we are discovering to our sorrow that the New Testament conception of church membership as a privilege rooted in sacrifice is nearer the truth. *The church is a communion, an all-pervasive, all-inclusive, all-demanding communion of men who determine to order their lives as best they can by the will of God as they see it in Jesus Christ.*

Obviously, the church so conceived is in a position of continual stress between the world in which it is and the vision of God's will for that world. It cannot help—and would not if it could—being an integral part of the total life of mankind. It registers our needs, desires, and aspirations. It is hindered by our prejudice, greed, passion, and ignorance. The wisdom of much of its program depends upon our wisdom and understanding, and these are inadequate at best. Its courage is always in proportion to the courage of the men and women who constitute its membership at any given time.

But the church can never be content to be a part of the total life of mankind, and nothing more. It is the mediator of that vision: "We beheld His glory as the only begotten son of God." This is the real source of the amazing vitality and unbreakable courage of the Christian church.

The purpose of the church as it seeks to relate this vision to life in a realistic manner has been neatly put by two discerning students, Arthur E. Holt and Dean Willard Sperry. Arthur Holt writes that, "The function of the Christian church is to maintain in contemporary society the passion of a redeeming God." [6] Dean Willard Sperry is in complete agreement: "The church's most important function is to make God real to every generation." [7] Methods of doing this have varied and will continue to vary, but that purpose will remain the same. The acid test of any part of our program and life is whether it helps make God real to this day. It is easy to appreciate the importance of the monastic movement to the Middle Ages and of revivalism to early American life because they helped to make God real to those ages. It is just as easy to appreciate the vast importance of a strong church school, a vigorous religious program on the college and university campus, an informed and interesting church press and radio program, an alert social action committee in the local church today—and for the same reason: they help make God real in terms of the needs of our day.

The great statesmen of the church are men who face forward, believing that the God of the past is God of the present and future as well, and that He has, in the words of the Pilgrim pastor, "more light to break forth from His word" and His world. Thus to face the future is not to ignore or depreciate the traditional and permanent functions of the church. Rather it assumes that the time-tested ways of awakening in men "the passion of a redeeming God" will be continued and strengthened in every known way. Worship, education, pastoral work, the administration of the sacraments—these are the day-to-day ways in which the church reaches out, trying to remold the misshapen spirits of men. Whatever we say is predicated on the assumption that these will continue to be the ordinary testimonies of the church to the extraordinary fact that "God was in Christ reconciling the world unto Himself."

But having taken due note of the importance and strength of traditional procedures, the fact is that the mark of vitality in religion is the effectiveness with which the church meets the special problems of any given age. By no stretch of our imagination can we, in any realistic way, face the special problems that confronted Christians in the days when imperial Rome hunted them in the Catacombs. We continue to be both thrilled and instructed by the glorious heroism which they wrote in the pages of "their time." Although we can and ought to face our problems in a spirit akin to theirs, our problems and theirs are utterly dissimilar in many important ways. It has always been so and, unless someone can find a way to throw history out of the gear of continual change, it will continue to be so. That is why, to adopt a truism, every generation of churchmen must be on their toes. No church can be so well established at any given time that its permanence is assured. As Ranke, the great German historian, observed, "Each generation lives directly to God."

> God hath anointed thee with odorous oil
> To wrestle not to reign!

III

We have it on good authority that "No man liveth unto himself." That, assuredly, is true of the church and her task. For the church, keeping watch over the well-being of men today, can no longer be likened to an isolated prophet, however great and compelling he may be, manning the walls of a city. Now it is many men in every race, nation, institution, and on every level of culture keeping ceaseless vigil over their flock. Nothing human is alien to their interest. They must look in every direction; they must communicate their discoveries to each other and to their people through many media including, of course, the personally spoken word.

Against this background of great need, it is easy to see why we ought to be everlastingly grateful for the sensitive spirits and alert minds of each generation who act as watchmen. Men like Walter Rauschenbusch, Shailer Mathews, Graham Taylor, Arthur Holt, and Reinhold Niebuhr are among those who, seeking to discern the signs of the times, have kept faithful watch over the welfare of this and the immediately preceding age. Like Jeremiah who prophesied a Scythian invasion that did not come off, they have been wrong often enough to demonstrate their humanity. But they have also been right often enough to convince any fair-minded person that they have learned in a marvelous way to think God's thoughts after Him. In these days of specialization we need some watchmen who can keep track of trends in various areas of life—men like Mr. James Myers in the field of labor relations. More than any other person in our day, he has helped the churches find their way toward a new and creative understanding of the spiritual values at stake in economic relations. When he speaks about such matters the church listens because it has learned to trust both his observations and his insight.

Courageous Christian journals like the *Christian Century* in this country and the *Christian Newsletter* in England, to mention but two, have rendered signal service to this day. Not being denominational in character, their space is largely free from the claim of organizational news and can be devoted almost entirely to the analysis of contemporary trends. To scan their files over the last several years is to view an incisive running commentary on the world issues that have been and are before mankind in general and the Christian faith in particular. They are always deep in controversy over vital matters; sometimes you are with them, sometimes against—but always the better informed for having read them. Excellent though these journals are, their kind is too scarce for the needs of the day. You cannot help wondering whether a great daily press under the auspices of the Protestant churches is beyond the realm of possibility. Certainly it suggests itself as one of the essential ways in which religion can exert a creative and continuous influence in public life and affairs. Obviously, it would be a costly matter in a day when you must have millions of dollars to finance such a venture, hundreds of thousands of subscribers to keep it going, and a large enough staff of thoroughly competent men to give it the expert guidance it would need. And, we must remember, sufficient freedom from bigotry and prudery to let it be a vital, interesting, and widely popular press. Religious journalism is in its infancy now and its proper growth should be the concern of a church determined to be a good watchman.

That the same considerations apply to the other great media for reaching public attention will be accepted as axiomatic. Radio, motion pictures, and theaters are just beginning to receive the attention they deserve from the institution which wants to be an effective influence for good in human life. One of the great seminaries of this country—the Chicago Theological Seminary—has for some years now been studying religious drama and encouraging its widespread use in churches. Recently, in collaboration with a major broadcasting company, it has begun a similar study of the effective use of radio by the church. Such developments occur in seminaries only when they first exist as felt needs in the life of the church. And their influence reaches far beyond the academic cloisters in which they are made, manifesting itself in a remarkable improvement in the quality of dramas and broadcasts sponsored by churches.

The relationship of the church to the motion-picture industry is far from satisfying, being, in effect, still in the "legion of decency" phase of censorship. I do not mean to decry the importance of this! Recently Mr. Eric Johnston, representing the motion-picture industry, solemnly assured a congressional committee that communism feared American motion pictures. He might have added that so does the Christian church, and any other institution interested in moral standards and stable human relationships and loyalties. Apparently the "legion of decency" is the most effective way of influencing Hollywood just now. If so, it deserves far more co-operation among Protestant Christians than it is receiving. But it is still an essentially negative approach and, if successful, does little more than cross out some of the wrong answers. It does not write in the correct ones.

Whether present ventures in religious films can perform this service or but serve as a spur in the proper direction to the great centers of the motion-picture industry remains to be seen. In any event, the church cannot be expected to adopt a do-nothing attitude toward the flood of films that, far worse than being poor entertainment, are obviously and blatantly immoral, no matter how leniently you define that word. When you consider how many people, especially children, are reached through this medium each day, you will be forced to wonder whether the church, as she values the future, has any more important task than helping the movies to discover the creative meaning of the moral law which lies at the heart of life and history.

Though we have our jokes at the expense of the numerous committees and boards of our churches, in our serious moments we thank God for them. When the war was yet young, the churches of America began to prepare for peace. They wanted the peace to be just and durable and, for it to be that, they knew it would need to be different from any peace ever before written. So they appointed a Commission on a Just and Durable Peace and asked it to guide their thinking in this matter. The commission met steadily and worked faithfully at its task of getting and keeping the problems of peace in proper perspective. Though the commission talked economics, race, education, tariff, reparations, colonies, etc., it never forgot that it was a group of churchmen, a group of men who were united, fundamentally, in rapt adoration of a vision. What they tried to do and are trying to do is to clarify the implications of the will of God as they see it in Jesus Christ for the problems of war, peace and world order. The work of the commission was closely watched not only throughout the church but also in the State Department and the Congress of the United States during the war. Its recommendations regarding peace have been widely circulated in the public press even though they have not been followed with any fidelity by the peacemakers to date. But the commission did bring the conscience of the church to that focal point of definiteness which was and is sorely needed in a time when peace-thinking and peace-making are of paramount public importance.

The work of commissions like this is an essential part of the life of an alert church today. There is no way of estimating our indebtedness to it and to other groups, like the Methodist Federation for Social Service and the Congregational Council for Social Action. They keep highlighting problems that ought to be pulled out of obscurity into the light of Christian conscience. We need not agree with their recommended courses of action in any given case in order to appreciate the fact that they have located vital issues. Here, as always, where human values are at stake, *it is better to be wrong than to be silent*. A wrong answer can be explained, but silence in the presence of injustice can never be explained. This fact alone places us in the continual debt of these vigorous groups. They deserve, not the caustic criticism of conservative churchmen, but the steady support of thoughtful Christian people. They deserve full meals at the table of denominational appropriations, not a few crumbs dropped from the table of this board or that.

The late Arthur E. Holt wrote the text for his own life and work in these words: "The field of social criticism and social action, since it is a part of life, is decidedly the province of an organization whose Master claims control of the whole of life." [8] Through his teaching and writings he established himself as one of the keenest and most dependable watchmen of the contemporary church. If I were asked to name one book which, better than any other published over the last decade, lays bare the spiritual need of the United States, it would be his magnum opus, *This Nation Under God*. In a calm, penetrating way he discusses the human meaning of democracy, why it is being challenged today, and how the Christian churches can help meet and master the competitors of democracy. If democracy should lose out here, I predict that, in the victors' orgy of book-burning, this would be one of the first books to go into the fire. But that fate is not to be feared so much as another—to be ignored or neglected by those of us who need to find solid spiritual foundations for our faith in democracy. A few years after it was published I asked the faculty of a college how many had read it. Only two responded. I asked how many knew of the existence of such a book. As many as half a dozen more were found. Almost all of them had read all or parts of *Mein Kampf*, and all knew of its existence. Yet scarcely anyone was familiar with one of democracy's deepest answers to *Mein Kampf*!

Books like Holt's volume reveal the Christian conscience at its best in its effort to achieve a new perspective. Two others, of more recent date, deserve to be associated with his great work. I refer to Professor M. Searles Bates's *Religious Liberty, an Inquiry* [9] and Dr. Paul Hutchinson's *The New Leviathan*.[10]

Professor Bates's book furnishes a new perspective on the world-wide problem of religious liberty. It deserves the careful attention of everyone who is interested in freedom of worship and who wants to know what the actual status of religious liberty

is all over the world at the present time. It paints a dark and forbidding picture, especially in the lands of Islam. The situation is
not much better in Latin America, Spain, and Portugal. Russia
and Mexico leave much to be desired. Storm signals are flying
here in America as a result of an aggressive effort on the part of
the Roman Catholic Church to become the dominant religious
institution in the thought and life of the governmental leaders of
this country. It is crystal clear from this careful study that religious liberty is no more assured now than it was before the recent war which was fought to win freedom of religion for
mankind. If anything, it is worse off.

Dr. Bates concludes in a vein reminiscent of Ezekiel, "These
are years of critical change, in which the patterns of destiny are
reshaped. Against the forces of oppression must be set the faith,
the determination, and the cooperation of uncounted millions
who in some form and degree value the potentialities of all mankind. The language of liberty, of peace, of democracy, of humanitarian goodwill, of religious faith, is here one. Let the cause of
religious liberty be fitly joined in the broader effort for the civil
and social liberties of men. Let the larger struggle for general
liberties enhance religious liberty among them." [11] We know
now that the whole notion of liberty, whether civil, social, or
religious, is wavering in the balance and that no one deed or
document is going to decide the issue for good or ill. As we
believe in the cause of liberty, books like these will find their
way into the press, pulpit, and programs of churches everywhere.
They deserve the careful attention of civic and educational leaders, of editors and businessmen, as well as of clergymen. The
warning word of a watchman like Professor Bates who discerns
danger ahead must be echoed by all watchmen until the city is
aroused and ready to defend itself.

Dr. Paul Hutchinson's book, *The New Leviathan,* is the most
disquieting study of the growing conflict between church and
state that has been printed to date. The author studies the emergence of the totalitarian state in the modern world. He traces the
development of its theory in the famous book by Thomas

Hobbes, *The Leviathan,* and the contradiction of that theory in the writings of John Locke. He points out that we have taken the course indicated in the writings of Locke rather than in the writings of Hobbes in the birth and development of political thought and life in this country. But, of late, a serious and studied change has come over our way of thinking about the fundamentals of our political and social life. This change is to swing from Locke to Hobbes in our political theory. The state here and everywhere today is becoming *The New Leviathan.* Dr. Hutchinson studies the new Leviathan at war, in peace, engaged in world-wide domination, in education, and in the control of all public centers of information. He shows that it is seeking to control schools, business, newspapers and radio, and, finally, the churches themselves. It acts as God; it sets up as its basic moral law its self-perpetuation; thus it flatly repudiates the God of historic religion. There can be no compromise with this modern Leviathan, Dr. Hutchinson warns. It must be fought by the church, and the battle is already well under way. The MacIntosh decision of the Supreme Court, the various decisions that have been rendered against Jehovah's Witnesses in these latter days—these are straws in the wind. Dr. Hutchinson suggests that the Christian church take up positions on these various points and be prepared to hold them to the end: (1) Remember that the church exists to proclaim the nature and will of the Christian God. This comes before everything else. (2) The church must keep itself free from any form of state subsidy or control. (3) The church must proclaim the end of the world of nationalism and the necessity for the transformation of our existing national loyalties into a globe-encircling loyalty to one world state. (4) The church must act as monitor of the state concerning the requirements of the moral law. Only thus can the state be kept humble before God rather than act as a proud god in its own right.[12]

This book places in clear perspective one of the great issues on which the church must now take the lead—if she values her historic mission and her freedom.

IV

One of the gravest issues on which the contemporary world must serve a new perspective is the meaning and use of power. We are talking power, thinking power, and preaching power these days. As we value our soul, we will mount the walls of the embattled human spirit and serve as watchman to the best of our ability on this matter.

Religion finds herself confronting an ancient task in this regard, a task that has grown harder rather than easier with the years. It is to persuade men that it is far safer to play with high explosives than to try to revise the affirmation "God is power" until it reads "Power is God." This, obviously, is a revision in words which amounts to a perversion in meaning. It is the studied opinion of religion that, as we love God, we who seek to be His servants will resist this perversion in meaning with every ounce of energy at our disposal. For if ever there was a short, well-paved road to ruin this is it: *power is God*. Yet, almost unconsciously, we have been brought to the point of accepting it as inevitable these days. And we have come to this decision by steps that are not hard to trace. We have been so occupied with the production and application of the instruments of power that we have either not had or not taken the time to reflect on the morality of power. Writers like Mr. Walter Lippmann, Bishop G. Bromley Oxnam, Mr. John Foster Dulles, and many others are telling us that power and responsibility go hand in hand for us today. They say that we must conduct ourselves, as a nation, in a manner befitting the greatest power on earth.

All of which points up the sharp fact that we must do some careful thinking about the nature and meaning of the kind of power we have, and relate it to God, in whose will we find our life, leading, and power. The idea of power, like the fabled nettle, must be gripped firmly in order to be held safely. It must be analyzed, understood, and accepted as an essential in life, though an essential that can easily become utterly destructive of the whole of life.

Fortunately, it is not hard to know what is meant by power in the claim that power is God. It means what Napoleon said it meant, that "God is on the side of the biggest battalions." Or what Machiavelli meant when he said that the only unforgivable sin in a ruler is to be weak. Power, so conceived, is composed of readily identifiable elements. It is composed of the abundance of material, resources, manpower, and engineering ability to create the weapons of war; of the ability of a nation to turn all its resources into the production of the equipment for and the waging of war; of the will to use this equipment with utmost vigor and with complete lack of moral scruples, looking only to complete military victory. Power, so constituted, is *coercive force*, being the ability to impose our will upon another as well as to prevent him from imposing his will upon us. It is the power of the centurion: the power to tell men to come and they come, to go and they go. No expense is spared in its creation and no limits are set upon its claim to the resources of life and society. In simple fact, as we have seen in recent history, the creation of the means of coercive force sooner or later becomes the central concern of all who place their trust in power, who believe that power is God. Believing this, they must place the whole of their life upon the altar dedicated to power!

If we who disbelieve that power is God are going to even hold our own, let alone win over those who so believe, we must be equally clear about what we mean by power when we say that God is power. We must make it clear that we are not opposing weakness to strength when we oppose God to the kind of power which man can create and control. Rather, we are opposing a greater strength to a lesser one. We must leave no one in doubt about the fact that we are not asking God kindly to excuse us from moral responsibility for action when we ascribe power to Him. Rather we are seeking how to stand with Him rather than against Him at those points where He seeks to work His will upon the world.

A good place to begin our study of the proper relationship between God and power is to note the fact that they are literally inseparable in the Bible. The Hebrews seemed utterly incapable of fathering an idea of God in which God is devoid of power. The Greeks could do this, but not the Hebrews. The Bible can be read as a record of the mighty deeds of God in the creation and history of the world; a God whose very word is so pregnant with power that it can create the heavens and the earth, and order them with seasons and people them with life; One whose will is empowered to create even the New Jerusalem, the Kingdom of God!

We begin with the impressive fact that there is complete agreement among the sixty-six books in the Bible on the claim that God is power: definite, decisive, irresistible power. But there the unanimity ends! A running argument rages over the question of the kind of power God has or is or exerts. The least we can say in deference to fact is that biblical thought about the power of God undergoes a long ethical and moral development.

The early Hebrews thought of His power as that of a god of war—Yahweh by name. He lived on Mount Sinai amid thunder and lightning—for these impressed all early peoples as immediate evidence of the presence and the power of God. Yahweh had stretched out his powerful hand to deliver the people from the tyranny of the most powerful ruler of the ancient world, a Pharaoh of Egypt. Moses, the servant of Yahweh, was endowed with the marvelous power that was essential to survival in the escape from Egypt and the sojourn of his people in the wilderness. But let Moses and the people lose faith in Yahweh's power, and it would strike them with the speed and terror of summer lightning. The power of God helped them to enter the Promised Land and secure control of it, so their chroniclers relate. It raised up mighty leaders like Saul, David, and Solomon who were symbols of Israel's greatness. They were powerful because the God who raised them up was powerful. Truly, he was the God of power.

The greatest difference between the earlier and the later Hebrew conceptions of the power of God is not simply a matter of time; it is a matter of morals. The early conception of power is essentially barbaric—clearly revealing the life of a primitive, nomadic people. It is swift, ruthless, capricious, vengeful. It strikes through storm, drought, famine, pestilence, and disaster generally. It is limited in scope but terrifying in its intensity. The God who wields it truly deserves the name coined by Bishop Francis J. McConnell: *God—the Almighty Smasher.* Distinctly, He is a God who makes you uncomfortable when He is around.

In later conceptions the power of God loses none of its original force, but it does gain the guidance of ethical principle. It becomes dependable, universal, and good. It wields punishment, yes, but punishment governed by justice. Even the punishments, themselves are clearly foreseen by the evildoer before he engages in the deeds which produce the punishment. The climax of Old Testament thought comes with the discovery that the finest expressions of the power of God are forgiveness and mercy. He strengthens His people: "They that wait upon the Lord shall renew their strength; they shall mount up with wings as eagles; they shall run and not be weary; and they shall walk and not faint." He becomes God the Father Almighty, one who can say, "Comfort ye, comfort ye my people. Behold the Lord God will come! . . . He shall feed His flock like a shepherd; He shall gather the lambs with His arm, and carry them in His bosom, and shall gently lead those that are with young." This moralizing of the power of God is one of the greatest achievements of the Hebrew religious genius.

The New Testament opens up to us our loftiest conception of the meaning of the power of God. What is the power of God like? It is like the growth of a mustard seed; like a bit of leaven in a bowl of dough. It works silently, steadily until it has exerted its will throughout the whole. Through whom or what does the power of God work? Not through thunder and lightning; not through fire falling from heaven; not through chasms to swallow up offenders. Does it work through princes and kingdoms? No! It works through little children, penitent publicans, the widow's mite—through humble, loyal people everywhere.

Those who expect a display of political pyrotechnics in the

New Testament conception of power are bound to be disappointed, but Paul was not disappointed because he sensed the real strength in the power of God so conceived: "God chose the weak of the world to shame the strong!" It is no accident that the writer of the Gospel of Matthew pictures the risen Christ saying to his disciples: "All power in heaven and on earth is given me! Go ye into all the world and lo! I am with you always!"

This is the tradition which speaks to and through us when we challenge the claim of many moderns that power is God and assert that God is power. It is a tradition which begins with God, the Smasher Almighty, and ends with God, the Father Almighty —a tradition which begins with God as a cosmic centurion pushing people around in an indiscriminate and barbaric way and ends with the persuasive power of Christ leading men to a new life. But this power of God is more than a tradition to be gloried in; it is a power to be experienced by every man on the face of the earth, by every nation that would live rather than die.

When the religious watchmen of our day bring news of this power to our beleaguered and troubled world, they must be prepared to face the question as to how and where men find this power of God which is so much stronger than any power man can make.

It is an open secret how men meet and avail themselves of this power of God.

The power of God is the power of truth. As we learned in grammar-school days, "Truth, crushed to earth, will rise again." Truth can be denied, deformed, distorted, ignored for awhile, but in the end it will rise in majesty to pronounce judgment upon its oppressors and to reign in triumph over them and what they planned to do in its absence or over its corpse. Truth is the power of God at work in the world, seeking to free men from their enslavement to greed, selfishness, passion, prejudice, and fear. The Christian says to the contemporary world, "You cannot go wrong on truth! It is one of the doors through which the power of God will come flooding into your life, remolding, redeeming, and transforming it. But you must open the door! Not even God can make you love and exalt the truth. You alone can do that. The door opens from the inside of your life and your times." This is strong doctrine to an age which has regarded truth as an instrument that it can employ at will in securing its way with other people.

The power of God is the power of goodness. It is not hard to sympathize with the excited college freshman in an ethics class who said, "Goodness isn't the least bit interesting or exciting!" I trust, however, that whoever thinks this way has had his fill of evil in these latter days. However interesting and exciting it may have been, it has been terribly tragic in character and cost. It is the steady conviction of religious faith that the power of God comes to us through the virtue of goodness. Goodness is no public or private parade of virtue, it is the sharing of life, in home, in community, in the world. It is a simple, near-at-hand, warmly human virtue. Yet it carries with it the power of eternity. Jesus was well aware of that fact. In fact he made it basic in his thinking and living. Can anyone read the Sermon on the Mount without suffering at least a twinge if not a stroke of conscience about his own conduct? There is something about the willingness to go the second mile, to turn the other cheek, to return prayers for curses that literally gets the conscience of men! In Mr. A. A. Milne's play, *Michael and Mary,* there is a probing scene between Michael and his father. They have been estranged for a long time but in Michael's hour of need his father comes to him—asking no questions, pointing up no morals—and makes available whatever he has to help Michael. Michael, weighing his father's act, says, "There is something about sheer goodness that gets me!" There is no real mystery about why it gets us. It is a cloak covering the power of God!

The power of God is the power of love. Love is not the sickening thing which we see so frequently in the motion pictures and read about in the pulp magazines. It is the simplest and deepest thing in life. It is the willingness to share the best we have and all we have without thought of restraint or reward. Love so conceived is of the essence of home and family, of genuine brotherhood among men, of the proper relationship with God. It is the most powerful force on earth. It is much stronger than any kind or amount of coercive power that men can gather together.

We let Napoleon testify earlier as to the power of the biggest battalions. He made that testimony when the biggest battalions were on his side. As long as they were there they did carry the illusion of omnipotence! But when they were dashed from his side and he stood alone on St. Helena, he said, "Alexander, Caesar, Charlemagne, and myself founded empires; but upon what did we rest the creation of our genius? *Upon force!* Jesus Christ alone founded his empire upon love; and at this hour millions of men would die for Him."

Love is stronger than hate—that is one of the observations which the watchman must drive home to the frantic spirit of the day in which we live. It is a definite and precise way of facing persecution and injustice, and a quite different way from that outlined in Paul Efrick Eldridge's poem, which attempts to express the feelings of Jews who have been hounded from Europe:

> This time we shall not forget—
> This time we shall not stretch our hand
> And offer "peace" to our foes.
> This time we shall build a raging fire
> Unquenchable
> Eternal
> Upon the altar of our hearts!
> This time we shall not forget! [13]

But love has another way of dealing with injustice and injury, a way prefigured in the words, "Father forgive them for they know not what they do!" In the midst of suffering, we are tempted to choose the path of hatred and vengeance but having glimpsed the divine meaning of love in Jesus Christ we, like Father Tyrell, feel, "Again and again I have been tempted to give up the struggle, but always the figure of that Strange Man hanging on the cross sends me back to my task again."

We who believe that God is power must keep ever before us the assertion that love is the supreme power of the Kingdom of

God! William Temple, Archbishop of Canterbury, said, "The Kingdom of God is the sovereignty of love, and the subordination of power to love is the principle of that Kingdom." To believe in love, to feel its power toward oneness is to live in the Kingdom of God even now. To be at one with man is to be at peace with God. To be at one with God is to be at peace with man. Let the religious watchmen tell a peace-hungry world that there is a road to peace but it is not the road of coercive power; it is the road of love.

The struggle between those who believe that power is God and those who believe that God is power is nearing its climax in these wild times. It is almost certain to be decided before our very eyes, within the fabric of our very life. And upon that decision hinges the destruction or the fulfillment of life. It is difficult to conceive of a more decisive age in which to live than this one. Those who believe that power is God are backing their belief with their time, effort, money, and their very life. Unless we who believe that God is power are prepared to give our faith the same kind of support, the decision is already in, even though the fury of the battle may be postponed for months, even years. But there is no cause to be fainthearted over the prospect. Other men in other ages have been asked to do as much as men of faith are asked to do today, and they have not been asked to do it alone, nor are we. As our faith in God is true, we stand at His side, and His cause will not fail.

V

It is only human to seek smaller tasks than these—they are almost too large for clear understanding, let alone effective action. We understand the program committee of a student conference when it requests a speaker to present "some little problems—ones we can do something about!" But, however human that impulse is, it would be suicidal for the Christian church to humor it now. We either tackle the big problems head on or accept immediate and irredeemable defeat for all that our Christian faith and culture have been striving for over two thousand years. I take it no one is ready to do this. Let us, then, in the spirit of eternal vigilance seek to be good watchmen of the eternal God, confronting our day with a new perspective on the deepest trends of the times, suggesting answers as well as raising problems.

LIBERALISM POINTS THE WAY *

I

There is something awesome about the definiteness of
the day in which we live. It is a grim truism to say that it is an
"either-or" rather than a "both-and" period in human history.
This fact has some very real advantages, though just now, and
for sufficient reason, its disadvantages seem to predominate. The
late Justice Holmes's summary of the way the Civil War affected
his youth gives us our best brief statement of the advantages of
living in such a day as this: "Through our great good fortune in
our youth our hearts were touched with fire. It was given to us
to learn at the outset that life is a profound and passionate thing."[1]
If fire is an agent of awakening, it is inconceivable that anywhere
on earth today any man is so dull as to be asleep. For we have had
enough judgmental fire rain down upon us to make the hells of
Dante and Milton seem like small bonfires for warming chilly
hands. And since the facile rationalizations by which men usually
live are among the most combustible of goods, the really worthy
views of life and goals for living have considerably less competition for public attention and favor than in the recent past. This,
I take it, is all to the good, and one of the advantages of living in
a day like this.

But the disadvantages of a time which insists on clear-cut definiteness, quick decision, and ruthless action are quite obvious and
well known. In fact, they add up to what Professor John McNeil

* The substance of this chapter was given as a lecture on the Ayer Foundation of the Colgate-Rochester Divinity School in 1944.

89

once called the "new age of barbarism." Dogmatism is one of the characteristics of our day: it is found in every confused area of life—race, economics, government, education, and religion. We in religion can speak with regrettable authority on the true meaning of dogmatism. It is a system which has built its walls so high that those on the outside cannot see in and those on the inside cannot see out. Dogmatism is able to bring order into life only to the extent that it is able to impose its ideology upon people. *Ideology*: there's a word for you! It, too, is characteristic of our day. Every movement must have an *ideology*. Now if we define this word by reference to actions, an ideology is a system with a club in its hand. It proposes to *get you* by persuasion if possible but, failing that, it will *get you* in some other way. The difference in ways of getting you being, of course, the slight difference between your life and your death!

Now it is the feeling of many of us that when we, collectively, have recovered to some extent from the recent mania for town-and-head smashing and the "liquidation" of opposition, we shall then look around for a saner way to live and, in so doing, will discover again the now neglected if not actually forsaken tenets of liberalism in philosophy, culture, and religion. And the reason for this feeling lies way beyond the reach of any such question-begging epithet as "wishful thinking." It lies both in the present status of liberalism in the world and in an appreciation of what liberalism has meant historically and what it can mean in the future. We who are "unashamed liberals" do not for one moment hold that the liberalism of yesterday was adequate in every way; we do say that it was looking and moving in the right direction. We do not say that historic liberalism made no major blunders in thought and policy; we do say that the spirit and objectives of historic liberalism were and are, in the main, right and that any age which thinks and acts otherwise will pay for its error in the "blood, sweat and tears" of ordinary people everywhere. The problem we are considering is not a cloistered concern. It did not arise in a cloister; it cannot be considered simply in terms of a cloister; and any answer we suggest will seek its validation in terms of purpose engendered in the daily life of ordinary people.

Today, liberalism is the whipping boy of several vigorous, yes, even intense and angry, movements. To begin with, all totalitarian movements single it out for special vilification. They scorn it for its lukewarmness, its deliberation, its confidence in man, history, and the universe. They curse it as "pink" when what they want is "red." Desiring to take their fate in their own hands, they seek to dismiss God and take over the running of their world.

Extreme conservatives—the very ones who are most afraid of the mass movements of the day—are scarcely less friendly to liberalism! They despise its open-mindedness, its willingness to reconsider old conclusions and policies in the light of new facts and interpretations, its readiness to embrace new conclusions if they are warranted. They know what they want and have no patience with anyone who even so much as intimates that what they want is either wrong or unattainable.

But it is when we step into the field of religion that liberalism is really taking a beating these days. Fundamentalism, orthodoxy, and neo-orthodoxy agree, so far as I can see, in just one thing: their scorn of liberalism. It betrayed the gospel, they charge. It believed in the delusion of automatic progress. It neglected the reality of evil and sin. It beclouded the clear-cut definiteness of historic theology—and in so doing it weakened the strong witness of the historic Christian faith at precisely that moment in human history when it was most needed. It encouraged an easy optimism about human life and history which are now plainly belied by historic facts. It came to terms with science, art, and philosophy and thereby, tacitly at least, surrendered the vantage point of sole supremacy as arbiter of truth and goodness in human life. Hence a great number of diverse religious movements are saying with varying degrees of emotional intensity that liberalism is a false messiah. And a surprising number of books are being written which assume that the matter is now closed, that liberalism is dead and awaiting only a decent public burial.

There are, however, several facts to be taken into account

before we proceed with this rite. The first of these is the presence
of liberalism in every vital historic religion. The second is the impressive list of achievements of liberalism in the Protestant tradition. And the third is a consideration of what liberalism in
religion means in terms of the emerging world.

II

Liberalism is far from being a peculiar Protestant phenomenon.
It is to be found in all the major religions of the Western world.
Judaism, for example, clearly exhibits both a conservative and a
liberal wing. The conservative or orthodox wing is by far the
larger numerically and, as its name implies, is primarily concerned
with keeping intact what is believed to be the inheritance of a
revealed and inerrant faith. The various subdivisions which occur
in orthodox Judaism stay within the limits of this common attitude. Liberalism, though outnumbered, is far from being out-
thought. It is present in the Jewish communities of Europe and
America and is easily the more aggressive group. The liberals
have been deeply influenced by the scientific, philosophical, and
social developments of the last four hundred years. They have
not been immune to influences from Christian theology. In fact,
they are rethinking and rewriting Jewish theology and ethics
under these powerful stimuli. They have excellent seminaries, and
their synagogues are led by men who are carefully trained to
interpret the traditions of their fathers in terms of the problems
of today.

The Roman Catholic Church is too complex and too contra-
dictory to be summed up in a sentence—even in one of Carl
Sandburg's three-page-long sentences. But this much can be said
with fairness: the Roman Catholic Church is not unfriendly to
liberal movements which will operate within the rigidly defined
limits of approved doctrine and polity. This gives greater latitude
for thought and action than might be apparent at first glance.
The famous encyclical of Pope Leo XIII *(Rerum Novarum)* on
the rights of labor in a modern industrial society threw open the

door to progressive labor movements under the aegis of the church. Catholics generally, have not chosen to walk through that door. In countries like Spain and in Latin America there is so close a relationship between church leadership and vested economic and political interests that the church is plainly and openly reactionary. But let it be noted, one of the most aggressive phases of a definitely aggressive Catholicism in the United States is the development of a liberal and progressive program for labor and agriculture.

Yet the Catholic Church will lay a heavy hand on any movement that insists on lifting the lids and having a look at the contents of church doctrines and dogmas. The modernist movement in evidence in Germany, France, and England throughout the nineteenth century was summarily dealt with and finally destroyed as a force in Catholicism at the turn of the century. This movement was the product of a liberalism that refused to observe what it regarded as arbitrary limits placed upon theological and philosophical thought. Its heresies are surprisingly orthodox to most of us: It insisted upon adopting the method and the findings of higher criticism in biblical research; it was friendly to the idea of separation of church and state; it embraced the findings of modern science; it championed public education under the guidance of secular governments; it accepted a belief in continuous revelation as over against a belief in the all-inclusive, all-sufficient, and historically fixed movement of revelation. The dire fate which overtook this liberal movement makes the outlook for any genuine liberalism in Roman Catholicism, as at present governed, extremely dark. But there will be recurrent tendencies in that direction—of that we may be sure. The Roman Catholic Church's historic genius for compromise and for smuggling the fruits of the heresy of one generation into the basket of the orthodoxy of the next gives some ground for the hope that the liberal effort of the last century will not be wholly lost even in Catholicism.

Liberalism has produced its largest, strongest, and most creative tradition in Protestantism. It is to this tradition that we now turn for a more intensive study of the meaning of liberalism as a force in human life and history.

III

There is reason to believe that the leaven in liberalism has been an active factor in Protestantism from the very beginning of its history. While it is not always easily identifiable in the tumultuous days of Luther and Calvin, it is nonetheless there and is a decisively important factor.

The early reformers themselves were liberals in a relative and limited fashion. Luther, for example, was a liberal relative to certain phases of Catholicism, i.e., the sacraments, celibacy, type of ecclesiastical polity, and the locus of authority. But he was anything but liberal in his view of the necessity of authority and of the Word of God as the fundamental authority of the faith. That is to say, Luther was a liberal so far as the medieval synthesis was concerned. Dr. Reinhold Niebuhr sums up the reasons for Luther's revolt in this illuminating paragraph: Luther was convinced "that no final peace could be found by the effort [of medieval Catholicism] to achieve righteousness. He had tried the method of monastic perfection and had failed. . . . He was convinced that the pretension of finality and perfection in the church was the root of spiritual pride and self-righteousness. His belief that the mystico-ascetic attempt at perfection was futile prompted his polemic against monasticism. His conviction that the pretension of finality was dangerous motivated his polemic against ecclesiasticism." [2] Having broken thus definitely with these fundamentals on the medieval synthesis, he moved on out into the new affirmations which constituted the genius of the Lutheran Reformation.

John Calvin was a liberal in this same sense, i.e., liberal as regards the medieval synthesis of Catholicism as well as various other reformation movements. But he was far from being even a limited liberal so far as his own formulations of the faith were concerned. He could not accept the implied, if not actually expressed, doctrine of assured righteousness through the efficacious mediation of the church. Righteousness, for him, cannot be assured for the good and sufficient reason that it cannot be attained. It was his confident judgment that "there still remains in a regenerate man a fountain of evil, continually producing irregular desires . . . that sin always exists in the saints until they are divested of their mortal bodies." [3] Having thus paved the way for a break with the authority of the church in matters pertaining to righteousness, he proceeds "to collect from various places in Scripture a rule for the reformation of life . . . ," as he himself says, and in so doing lays the foundations of legalism and moralism which have been at once the strength and the weakness of Calvinism as a theology and an ethic. But the point I am making just now is that he, as well as Luther, began by registering a vigorous dissent from certain fundamentals in a hitherto accepted religious tradition. Then he, like Luther, pushed ahead to the task of reformulating the entire Christian tradition along new as well as old lines. Neither one regarded himself as doing other than providing a more effective vehicle for Christian truth to be presented to man.

It is possible, I believe, to discern in men like these and in the historic movements which they set off four well-defined stages in the development of liberalism as a definite tradition in Protestantism.

The first stage is the one in which there occurs the fact of a vigorous dissent from some of the fundamentals of the accepted religious tradition. This dissent may be based upon mystical experience which encourages the recipient to believe that it should take precedence over the authority enshrined in tradition. Or it may be based upon a new interpretation of the Scriptures or the sacraments or some other part of the apparatus of accepted authority. Or it may be based upon some philosophical or cultural movement of dissent, like the Renaissance, which moved upon the medieval synthesis on a broad front. The starting point of liberalism in religion is the historic event in which dissent from the established tradition arises *within that tradition itself*.

The second stage in the development of liberalism sees the fact of dissent making good its right to live. This is no easy matter. The forces behind tradition are usually powerful, and they are called upon at once to deal with any threat to unity. Reason and persuasion will undoubtedly be tried at first. But, should these fail, disciplinary measures are sure to be evoked. Finally, the combined weight of the entire social structure which embraces the accepted religious tradition is brought to bear upon the "menace." If these measures are successful (and they usually are, historically speaking) that ends the matter—for the time being. But where they are not successful, where the fact of dissent is able to rally sufficient force of one kind or another to establish the right to be heard, there we have a liberal tradition under way. Various dissident movements in the Reformation period sought and found different kinds of support: some had the support of the state; some created a congenial civil power which in turn was dependent for its support upon the religious movement itself; some sought out a new world where they could proceed without overt conflict with the established religious tradition. But, by one means or another, the fact of dissent must make good its right to reformulate the established religious synthesis if it is to live and perpetuate itself as a religious tradition.

The third stage in the development of a liberal tradition in religion is one in which the fact of dissent produces its own formulation of the faith, i.e., its own theology and philosophy as well as its own organization and program. Dissent may and does begin as an inspired protest but, if it is to live, it must finally become a definite, creative, organized movement and, with the passage of time, a religious tradition in every sense of that term. Obviously there will be much fumbling around for the theological formulations and the type of organization which will do the greatest justice to the inspired protest. Many will be tried but few will survive the testing fires of historical experience. It is in this stage that dissent becomes both self-conscious and conscious of history and seeks to relate itself to the entire corpus of human knowledge and the entire range of human experience, becoming thereby a dynamic force in history.

The fourth stage, of course, is the culmination of all that has gone before. In it dissent finally becomes a full-bodied, positive religious tradition; it becomes an accepted fact and factor in the life and history of a community or, if it is a wide-sweeping movement, of a society. It will have real status in the law and the conventions of the society in which it flourishes. Its moral principles will be reflected in some definite way in the social controls of custom, convention, and government. Consider, as an example, this remark of one politician in Virginia to another, relative to a certain proposal: "The Baptists won't stand for that!" Or *Time* magazine's verdict on the action of a church conference in supporting the United Nations Organization: "The largest body of churchmen in the United States plumped squarely behind the Dumbarton Oaks Proposals for world organization."

These are illustrations of the way in which a religious tradition is recognized in a thoroughgoing realistic way. When liberalism becomes a tradition, its philosophy and theology will be influential factors in shaping the educational ideals and practices of the social order. Witness the way in which the church-supported and church-related academies and colleges and universities spread across this country in the last century, anticipating and setting many of the standards for the great public school system which later was to grow up and take over the task of educating the citizens of this particular social order. When facts like these are in evidence in the history of a religious movement, we are justified in concluding that what began as an inspired protest has finally become an established tradition.

The historical achievements of liberalism in the Protestant tradition combine to write a record of which we can well be proud. What it has either done or helped do in the field of biblical research, theological fecundity, the social-gospel movement, and the encouragement of the growth of democracy looms so large in any formulation of contemporary Protestantism that it must be regarded as essential in it. Even a hasty view of these great achievements is rewarding.

Biblical research was forced upon Protestantism when the great reformers shifted the base of authority in religion from the church to the Scriptures. There is an interesting prefiguration of this shift in the experience of first- and second-century Christians when they broke with Judaism yet retained the Jewish Scriptures. In both periods the precursors of the new faith accepted the inherited Scriptures as infallible—until they settled down to the hard task of studying them! The problems they encountered were both numerous and staggering. The keener students were always on the threshold of that ecclesiastical doghouse called heresy. Only an elaborate and labored use of analogy and allegory kept most of them out of it! Following the Reformation, or really in the latter part of Luther's own lifetime, the study of the Bible was broken down into the study of the Old and the New Testaments. Then, in turn, each of these was broken down for study into its various books. Then, inevitably, the documents in each book (where there are such) were distinguished and interpreted. Always there were the problems of manuscript, of translation, of authorship. Though set in motion by the Reformation as a special and significant discipline, biblical research has had to fight for its very life within Protestantism itself. The forces of fundamentalism have rightly feared its growing influence and have sought to curb its freedom of inquiry. Fortunately, biblical study has kept on its course and is stronger today than ever before.

The theological fecundity of liberalism is usually singled out as one of its major weaknesses. Its almost infinite variety is compared, and usually unfavorably, with the monumental system of Thomism. I propose to treat this diversity as a virtue, a strength, because of what it has meant to the virility of Protestantism. Once the reformers had set the precedent of questioning some of the fundamentals of the medieval synthesis their disciples were encouraged to do likewise even as regards some of the new fundamentals introduced by the reformers themselves. The upshot of this was and is that no theological position is too hallowed to be questioned. If Luther could question the validity of the doctrine of transubstantiation, his spiritual descendants were at liberty to question his doctrine of consubstantiation. If Calvin could deny that the church can guarantee salvation through sacramental efficacy, then his spiritual heirs could and did modify, if not actually discard, his doctrine of predestination. If Wesley could challenge the pessimism of the early reformers with his doctrine of perfectionism, his latter-day followers need feel no compunction about curbing the idea of perfection by linking it securely with the reality of moral evil and the ever present reality of sin in the life of good men. That each generation of liberals has had to fight for this freedom is a small matter. One of their most effective weapons has been and is the appeal to the behavior of their spiritual parents. And, as any father can testify, that sort of appeal brings the argument to an abrupt end!

It was this precious tradition of the intellectual freedom of dissent which made it possible for liberal Protestant thinkers to effect a *rapprochement* with the powerful philosophical and scientific developments over the last two hundred years. Here again, it is easy to appear to be claiming too much. There can be no denial of the admission that many serious mistakes were made in this process. When romanticism was the dominant mood of philosophy, theology was preoccupied with feelings and sentiments to the ominous exclusion of reason and moral values. When a mechanistic naturalism dominated philosophy, many religious thinkers made almost uncritical terms with it, surrendering, in effect, the notion of the soul as the gift of God to every man, and of religion as the precious personal experience of the divine. Despite mistakes like these—which were repudiated in short order— the net effect of this exercise of intellectual freedom created in Protestantism a new sense of the relevance of religion to the entire human enterprise. Thus a new confidence in the individual and in society was brought to birth. The dark pessimism about man and the world, so characteristic of the Middle Ages and the reformers themselves, was considerably—and, as it now appears, prematurely —lightened by the notion of man's intrinsic goodness. Dr. A. C.

McGiffert is correct in saying that early American liberalism affirmed its "faith in the worth and dignity of man, together with a correlative denial of total depravity and unconditional election." [4] Although evangelical sects continued to sing, "I am a stranger here within a foreign land; my home is far away beyond a golden strand," a sense of at-homeness in this world was being engendered by the conviction that God was seeking to work a mighty work in and through men who, by an act of faith in Christ, become co-workers together with Him in the building of His Kingdom.

The forces of liberalism in Protestantism unhesitatingly took sides in the conflict between the otherworldly and the at-home tendencies in religion—and out of their united and persevering efforts came what is popularly known as the *social gospel*. Under the vigorous leadership of men like Rauschenbusch, Peabody, Mathews, Lyman, and many others, it brought into being an effective alternative to both the otherworldliness of popular Protestantism and the individualism of much if not most of the eighteenth and nineteenth centuries' thought and culture. So far from being gullible optimists and credulous believers in automatic progress, these men were keenly aware of the reality of sin and evil in personal and social living. No man in his day, or ours either, had a clearer picture of the reality of social sin and titanic social evils than did Walter Rauschenbusch. I have yet to meet a man more sensitive to the contradictions between good and evil in individuals and institutions alike than Shailer Mathews. It was the liberal forces in Protestantism which threw their support behind men like these and helped spread their influence throughout the entire Protestant tradition. The flowering of realistic social creeds in most major Protestant denominations is directly attributable to their creative potency. This fact is all too frequently overlooked or undervalued when some of our contemporaries get warmed up to the task of berating liberalism.

If liberalism did one thing which more than any other encouraged the growth of democracy, it was to shift the emphasis in morality from *obedience* to *responsibility* in matters of religious thought and life. Obedience is the watchword of hierarchies, of kings and emperors, of masters. You can build a morality upon it, but it will be a morality which functions from the top down—with leaders acting as head, conscience, and will for the whole body. Responsibility is the watchword of democracy, placing as it does the full thrust of common social life upon the individual, requiring of him that he exercise his mind, his will, his judgment before the social body can act. A morality built around responsibility is bound to exhibit more confusion, to be slower to start and harder to stop than an obedience morality. But it will have the advantage of operating from the bottom up and being able to command the support of the people.

"Consent of the governed" is the essential of democratic government. "For the general welfare" is the highest legal standard of justice in a democracy. "The right of trial by a jury of one's peers" is the essential court procedure of a democracy. "An educated and informed citizenry" is one of the necessary goals of a democracy determined to live. I do not claim these as the fruits of religious liberalism alone, for many other factors went into their creation. But I do say that the forces of liberalism in religion rendered invaluable assistance in the creation and nurture of these ideals to their present status in our common civic life. And if democracy is not to collapse into a conglomeration of quarreling pressure groups it will be because religious liberalism, among other forces and factors, has succeeded in training people to think about and work for the common good.

IV

Now, against this historical background, it is possible to attempt a somewhat exact description of liberalism. Obviously it is not a creed separate and distinct from other creeds; nor is it a peculiar ethic, much less a separate organization within a religious tradition though, as we have seen, it acts like a leaven within a tradition.

Liberalism is a philosophy of history which holds that the human enterprise is the scene of the constant activity of God and that God's will can therefore be sought and found in history. God is the Creator, Sustainer, and Redeemer of the world, including the human race. God is the continuing Fact and Factor for good in human life. Liberalism does not and is not concerned to deny the possibility that there has been at some point in history a *special revelation* of God's will. But it does object when this claim either explicitly or implicitly reduces all subsequent history to a place of minor importance in understanding the will of God. It, liberalism, is friendly to the debatable notions of continuous revelation as well as progressive revelation, though it does not nail its banner to the mast of either. But it does see in them earnest attempts to take all history seriously, as befits its view of the relationship between God and history.

Liberalism is a view of truth which holds that truth is one, united and infinite, being in fact God's will for the world. Our grasp of truth is partial and fragmentary at best. It will never be complete because that which is finite cannot hope to comprehend that which is infinite. For liberalism there are many roads to truth: that of the seer, the prophet, the artist, the scientist, the thinker, the social engineer. It is permissible to speak of various roads to truth but not of various kinds of truth, i.e., religious truth, scientific truth, philosophic truth. Liberalism's conception of truth imparts the spiritual unity of a common goal to the otherwise scattered creative enterprises of the human spirit. It fosters a sense of humility about one's own efforts and achievements. It creates a sense of comradeship with the other forces which are seeking the common goal of a better understanding of life and the world.

Liberalism, in short, is the vital edge of creative, reverent religion. It is not a separate religion. It is to any given religious tradition what the frontier is to the settled areas of a country. Each is essential to the growth and eventual security of the other. A liberal in religion will share most heartily in most of the theology of the conservative. Many if not most of their disagreements will deal with details rather than fundamentals, though, as we have seen, there is always the likelihood of disagreement here also. The point at which they will not see eye to eye is on any given formulation of the faith. The conservative will want to insist upon such as fixed and final and worthy of all acceptation; the liberal will defer his judgment until he has studied the biography of the statement as a whole and of its various parts. For he knows that it will have such a biography; every creed in Christendom does have one and cannot be understood apart from it. How the conservative can therefore placidly insist that the creed "as is" shall be taken as the measurement of faith is more than the liberal can understand—or will accept.

In taking this critical attitude toward the great heritage of religion, the liberal does not forswear faith as an active element in religion. Faith, for him, is not knowledge in advance of experience; neither is it knowledge in defiance of reason and experience. Rather it is the projection of his life along a pathway of action which definitely runs beyond his knowledge and experience. Believing in God as he most devoutly does, this sort of adventuring is not groping in the dark; it is an earnest and persistent attempt to link his life's course with the will of the Creator as that will conditions the future. So far from being a man of little faith, the liberal is a man of great faith—or he soon ceases to be a liberal! Were it not for him, the first creed would have been the final creed of our faith. He is the one who demands that inherited formulas be modified in the light of the growing experience of religious persons. He does not shrink from using the historic creeds of the church as great statements of the essential faith of the Christian religion. But he never loses sight of their ancestry; he never lets them become short cuts to a hard-won faith of his own. The conservative spirit in religion treats some one creed or other as a figurative Mount of Transfiguration and calls loudly that houses of faith should be built thereon, wherein the faithful may stay; the liberal spirit knows that, precious as is the vision, it leads straight down the mountainside into the unfinished work and history of mankind.

How, then, does liberalism in religion point the way for the emerging world? Let me specify briefly five contributions which it can be counted upon to try to make.

1. Liberalism will be the champion of tolerance, a tolerance based upon convictions held in all sincerity and humility. It will struggle against intolerance in thought and action which is so dangerous a threat to an orderly and peaceful future. The importance of this contribution is too obvious to require much emphasis. It ought to be clear now that the fundamental freedom in human affairs is freedom of religion. If, or to the extent that, this is assured, the other precious freedoms (of press, assembly, information) are attainable. We cannot begin by coercing the mind and conscience of men in religion and end up with anything other than a form of fascism. Men must be free, and equally free, to worship God or not worship God, as they please. To be sure, this position may be abused, may lead to great danger, but it is much to be preferred to the dangers which threaten in any alternative view. Hence, liberalism cannot accept the Roman Catholic doctrine of religious toleration in virtue of which non-Catholic religions live in obscurity and on sufferance of the Catholic hierarchy—much as the evangelical churches now exist in Spain! Liberalism ranges itself against such proceedings not merely because of creedal differences with Roman Catholicism but even more deeply because toleration, so conceived, is not freedom; it is a form of serfdom. Liberalism takes seriously the necessity of complete freedom of religion as a prerequisite of an orderly and peaceful world. It insists that every faith is thereby granted its God-given right of diffusion through persuasion. It grants no other means to any faith.

2. Liberalism will strive for a growing unity among the many sects of Protestantism. It is interesting to note the fact that the divisions in Christendom are a scandal only to liberalism. To be sure, the major churches deplore the errors of everyone else, and periodically send out the invitation to "come over and be right with us!" Liberalism insists that this attitude is just as indefensible and as utterly unnecessary as are the divisions themselves. The

main reasons which led to the divisions among us belong, for the most part, to the ages; they are not living issues now, except as ignorance and intolerance let them live. Liberals in every group are working for the kind of church unity which may and will begin as co-operation but which aims at union as surely as the sun rises and sets.

3. Liberalism will work for a growing co-operation among the religions of the world. It will neither be deterred by the cry that this is treason to the Christian cause nor be discouraged at the enormous obstacles to be overcome before the religions of the world learn the ways of peace with and among each other. So far from being treason the strategy of co-operation is the only one that can be justified by reference to Christian ethics. As we believe in one God, the Lord and Father of all men, revealed to us supremely in Jesus Christ, the Saviour of all men, we will leave no stone unturned in our effort to become better acquainted with all other religions. Some of the most serious obstacles to co-operation are encountered at the outset of our contact with other faiths. Missionaries know this better than anyone else can ever hope to know it. The Buddhist, for example, is not only hostile to Christianity, of which he knows next to nothing, but very suspicious of the ultimate designs of Christians—which, of course, is a tragic commentary on the total impact of Western culture upon the Orient. Fortunately for the cause of co-operation, the missionary program, especially through the growth of the indigenous churches, is winning the kind of confidence which can result in the growth of genuine co-operation. One of the things that slows up co-operation is the fear on the part of our more liberally minded missionaries that such activities will be misunderstood at "the home base." It is at precisely this point that the influence of liberalism can be most useful to the cause of co-operation among the religions of the world. To the challenge that this is dangerous because it may result in fundamental changes in the Christian faith, the answer must be made that (a) no change will be sprung on us or anyone else unawares; there will be ample opportunity to "live" with it long before it becomes an accomplished historical

fact; (b) the principle implicit in the challenge would have kept Christianity as a sect within Judaism if the Christians of the first two centuries had not had the courage to steer their faith through changes in fundamental formulations that were at least as serious as any we might conceivably be called upon to encounter. Liberalism believes in the activity of God in history, and it is willing to leave the issues of any serious and sustained attempt at co-operation in His hands. Men whose faith is limited to their creeds may and will shrink away from the possibility of basic change, but the liberal has learned his history too well to believe that God has ceased revealing Himself to men through the ongoing processes of history. The liberal will seek therefore to bring all men into some kind of co-operative relationship through which God's one will and truth can speak to all men.

4. Liberalism will seek a spiritual unity among the creative efforts of men. It will try to bring to an end the blight of condescension which can all too readily be seen in the usual approach of religion to the disciplines of art, science, philosophy, social service, and education. I say "blight of condescension" advisedly, because religion usually, and tacitly, assumes that what it is talking about is infinitely more precious than anything else that others may be concerned with. This attitude is more than infuriating; it is unjustifiable. If God be One, if truth be One, if truth be the way to the good life, then whoever serves the truth in any area of life serves God as truly as anyone else in any other area. Liberalism regards religious revelation, scientific discovery, and aesthetic insight as types of interaction with God and truth. This is not to say that they are alike in procedure, or in their demands upon men—that obviously is not true. But they are ways in which man encounters truth, the truth of God, and none are "common or unclean." Paraphrasing the astronomer's dictum, "No one observatory is adequate to the tasks of astronomy," the liberal says, "No one way of apprehending truth is adequate to the total richness and meaning of God's truth." That is why liberalism continues to work steadily at the task of bridging the fissures which conservatism seems to delight in opening up between religion and

science, religion and education, religion and art, religion and all other creative essential disciplines. Not only does religion suffer the fate of declaring itself, by implication at least, to be irrelevant to these great concerns, of being walled off from the areas where so much of the world's work goes on, but also it gives the impression to conscientious workers in these areas that what they are doing is of secondary importance—an impression that is rightly resented. Liberalism seeks a different approach to the matter; it seeks to put an end to the condescension which so frequently masquerades as conviction; it proposes to present religion as the unitive bond among the creative interests and work of society, to treat all sincere workers for the welfare of mankind as ministers of His will.

5. Liberalism will nurture a new confidence in man. We sorely need it! It is well to recall Canon F. R. Barry's observation that "Christianity was born into a world that was haunted by the conviction that man was about played out." [5] Christianity countered with the assurance that each man is infinitely precious in the sight and plan of the God of the universe. This assurance was translated into a fellowship and a conviction of work to be done, of life to be lived in a certain way. Thus the battle over pessimism was won, and thus it can be won again in the twentieth century when, once more, men are losing faith in the human enterprise. Conservative religion need not be blackly pessimistic, as so much of it is, in order to be faithful to the realism of the Christian gospel. Sometimes it seems to go to the extreme of forgetting that God thought man worthy of salvation! Liberalism approaches modern man with no new message. It brings the great assurances of the classic tradition in Christian thought. It preaches the time-tested gospel of the proper relationship between man and man, and man and God, of the reality of sin and evil in human life and the reality of God's forgiving love as revealed in Jesus Christ, of the church as the fellowship of those who accept the Lordship of Christ, of the necessity of living each day in the light of his life and teachings, of the assurance of strength sufficient for every trial, even the trial of death.

No man can hold these convictions and be an all-out pessimist about the human enterprise! Yet they must be translated into concrete relationships in home, in school, in church, in civil and international affairs. They cannot long endure separated from the crushing work and problems of the world. That is why liberalism knows no easy road to the restoration of confidence in man and society. So far from being committed to the notion that an escalator-like progress is inevitable in human affairs, liberalism asserts that progress is possible if man will take seriously the Christian view of life, if man will live and act as befits a responsible creature of God. How far we can actually remold the structure of human society on the pattern of the Kingdom of God depends more upon what God will permit than upon what man may design. But there is no other way of learning what He will permit than of planning and working for the achievement of the highest we know. To the challenge so frequently put to the liberal: "Do you believe that the Kingdom of God can actually be built here?" the liberal replies, "Yes, in so far as God will permit it to be built!" Liberalism is not "just a social philosophy"; it is a religious view of social responsibility, one according to which all that men plan and do is planned and done under the eye of the God of all creation, whose will will have the last word on all our plans and attempted achievements. The intense social passion of liberalism accepts with reverence the profound truth: "Except the Lord build the house, they labour in vain that build it: except the Lord keep the city, the watchman waketh but in vain."

Thus liberalism holds before man a destiny couched in terms of divine duty. Man can become a co-worker with God in the building of the good society, the Kingdom of God—this is his highest destiny. Man should accept this destiny and commit himself to its realization both personally and socially—this is his divine duty.

I

How eagerly we grasp, how easily we use, and how inevitably we misuse such fine phrases as "the century of the common man"! Not many conversations about social problems these days proceed far without invoking "the average man." Yet such designations are used with so many different shades of meaning that they become little more than slogans. And a slogan, we have been reminded, "is a catchword to deliver the unwary into the hands of the unscrupulous." Not wanting to endure that fate, I propose that we begin by paying strict attention to the phrase "the common man."

It seems to carry two types of meaning: (1) all men; (2) the rank and file, the "ordinary" or "average" man. In the first sense, it is an inclusive concept; in the second, it is a divisive one, applying to one portion of mankind as over against the rest. In the latter meaning it is always necessary to state the differential, which may be degree of education, amount of wealth, relationship to distinguished ancestral lines, etc. When such differentials are used as lines of division between men, "common man" always denotes the man who does not enjoy the advantages indicated in the differential. Both meanings of the phrase are in current usage, and both supply significant approaches to this study of the church's especial responsibility for "the common man." Let us consider them in turn.

If we take the inclusive meaning of "the common man," "the century of the common man" indicates a century in which the needs of all men are understood and accepted as objects of shared effort, and are met evenly and as adequately as it is now possible to meet them. It means, in effect, a century of the common good. This observation, however, is an introduction, not a conclusion, to our task. For it lays us under immediate obligation to inquire after the basic needs of all men which must be met before the goal of common good can be achieved. What are the minimum requirements for living that are implicit in the fact of life itself? Such, surely, will be enjoyed by all men everywhere in an era dedicated to the common good.

The initial step toward any adequate answer must specify such essentials as food, shelter, clothing, work, recreation, social recognition, opportunity for new experience, and a sense of unity with some social group. So far as we know, there can be no question as to whether such needs are actually *basic* for all men. This is not to say that because all men *need* food with certain nutritional values all men will *want* it, or that all will want their vitamins presented in the same way! Variations in form, manner, and custom will appear with the various cultural levels and groupings of mankind. But that such needs will seek expression and finally be a decisive factor in determining the character of all such levels and groupings is not open to serious question. The way in which art, science, and religion, historically, have both grown from and been intimately interrelated with the food-gathering activities of mankind warns us not to treat them as things apart from such interests even today.

A second step toward determining the basic needs of all men is dictated by the fact that man is a social being. Not only is his body the product of the union of his parents, but, in addition, his habits, language, loyalties, and standard of values are, initially at least, the product of his social environment. As a social being, man needs understanding, fellowship, respect for tradition, respect for the integrity of others, a sense of loyalty to causes which concern the welfare of the group, and a willingness to assume responsibility in group life. The group orders itself by some form of government, perpetuates itself by some form of education of its young, and secures itself by every known means against all threats to its welfare. The individual man is always involved in these indispensable group activities, and they must be regarded as being among his essential needs since they are basic to the group life which he needs.

A third step must be taken in arriving at an adequate notion of what constitutes the basic needs of man. It is to realize his need for a consciousness of a secure relationship with the supernatural, or at least superhuman, power or powers whose activities he sees throughout the whole range of life. That this is the taproot of religion is at once apparent. Man's thought about God has varied and continues to vary. But, by and large, there is no variation in the fact that man feels himself to be a part of a universe with which he must make some conscious and responsible form of adjustment. His effort to satisfy this need shows itself as an essential complement of all his practical activities. Incantations, charms, and prayers accompany the sowing of the seed in primitive religion—and they are regarded as of equal importance in securing a bountiful crop. This primitive belief has persisted in some guise in even the most sophisticated forms of modern religion. It is an expression of man's need to feel at home, we say, in the universe. Modern man needs this as badly as early man, however different his manner of meeting the need may be.

These three categories of basic needs are not presented as being sharply set apart from each other. Man, as a psychophysical organism, has certain needs. The further fact that he is a social being adds other needs. And the distinctive fact that he is a spiritual being, a person, adds still other needs. Yet these various levels of need, though they may be noted separately for purposes of clarity in understanding, never occur separately in human life, being bound in an organic unity in the fact of personality. Insofar as man's life seeks fulfillment through a meeting of these needs, he is endowed with dignity or consciousness of meaning and worth, which must be regarded as one of the characteristics of the good life.

The Christian church, interested as it is in the whole man as well as the whole of mankind, must begin its thinking about a century for the common man, and its striving to make it a century of the common good, with a recognition of these needs which bind all men into one bundle of life. The church must study how she can more adequately define her activities in terms of such needs; she must take upon herself the mantle of being that institution which is primarily dedicated to the task of stimulating men until international, economic, and social conditions permit a general fulfillment of them.

If the afore-mentioned needs were *evenly met among all men*, there would be no occasion to consider the second general meaning of the phrase "common man." This, as was noted in the introductory paragraph, is a divisive meaning in that it is based upon the existence of divisions among men, with the dividing line being some differential or other. A vivid picture of this meaning in history is found in an earlier division of men into royalty, nobility, gentry, and peasantry. To name them in this order is to move from the apex of the pyramid to its base, numerically speaking, i.e., from the few to the many. It is also, paradoxically enough, to move from greater to lesser power and privilege. The differentials which supported this division among men might be lineage, wealth, or sometimes stark power, but in every case they conferred their favors upon the few and their exactions upon the many.

The general differential that throws more light upon the problems of our day than any other is drawn by the degree to which the needs common to all men are either met or unmet. On one side of the dividing line of human need are the "privileged," on the other side, the "underprivileged." The privileged are those whose education, income, position, culture, and power combine to yield at least a great measure of confidence in themselves and of security for themselves and their families for the future. It may be said, in general, that their basic needs are amply provided for; their source of income has the stable protection of existing law and order and can be maintained by their industry. The underprivileged are those who lack all or most of these personal and social assurances. In this group we find the hundreds of millions of persons who live in the cloud of ignorance. Lacking knowledge of the laws of health, they are victimized by diseases which could be prevented by proper foods. Lacking knowledge of different grains and crops, and their proper rotation, they do not draw from the soil the kind of healthful sustenance which it could provide. Lacking knowledge of mineral deposits and other potential sources of trade, they are unable to institute commercial relations with other sections of the world that would supply the necessary goods which may be lacking in their locale.

Also among the underprivileged must be numbered the millions of persons in our and other lands who have been unable to get a secure economic foothold in the social order. The glib criticism that "such persons are lazy or undeserving" can be set to one side until it is demonstrated that the existing order has a place for them commensurate with their dignity as human beings. The stark fact must be faced that nearly one-half the population of the earth lives at a barely subsistence level even in peacetime. It is safe to say that for such peoples there is as yet no security whatever so far as basic livelihood is concerned. When Mr. Carr writes, "Not poverty but unemployment is the scourge of our social system," [2] he is talking about the modern industrial system of the West. Among the large population groups of the Orient, as among the native peoples of Africa and a large proportion of Latin Americans, *poverty*, not unemployment, is the scourge of human existence. To single out poverty as the crippling fact in India, for example, is not to gloss over, much less ignore, other grave social problems, like *caste*, which multiplies the effects of poverty a hundredfold by making it appear to be a normal part of man's destiny in this life.

The rank political, economic, and educational injustices inflicted upon millions of Negroes and sharecroppers in the United States should remind us that we are talking about concrete problems close at home as well as grievous ones in other lands. These large population groups find their roads toward the good life blocked by gates that are barred by social convention and, in many cases, discriminatory legislation.

Another numerous underprivileged group is to be found in the large industrialized and urban areas of the world. For lack of a commonly accepted designation, let us call them the slum dwellers. Undernourishment, congested housing conditions, inadequate sanitary provisions, juvenile delinquency, crime among youth and adults, epidemics, low moral standards, low incomes, economic insecurity, inadequate churches and schools—these are the dark realities which cast their shadow over the slum dwellers. Making due allowance for artistic hyperbole, John Steinbeck's *Grapes of Wrath* and Richard Wright's *Native Son* outline a true picture of the meaning of underprivilege in human life.

That major social dangers are inherent in the existence of large groups of underprivileged peoples is clearly revealed (1) by the emergence of dictatorships and (2) the recognition they have been receiving in the social legislation of every nation in the world. When underprivileged groups are aware of the injustice of their plight, the appeal of the demagogue falls on eager ears. We must recognize the truth of Mr. Peter Drucker's assertion: "Any society which cannot prevent the development of masses is irrevocably doomed." Fearful of this, we in the United States have spent billions of dollars over the past decade in a series of efforts to reduce unemployment, raise the lower income brackets, and provide a minimal security for all men. England has gone much farther, so far in fact that the "old England" of accepted social inequities is dying if not dead. In December, 1942, England was confronted by the Beveridge Plan, which "rang out the old, rang in the new" of widespread social change in English life. Its revolutionary implications were clearly seen at once. Upon its presentation to the public, *The Spectator* carried this editorial comment: "It now remains for the Cabinet, the House of Commons, and the country to grasp or to reject the opportunity of securing to every citizen of the land, through all the vicissitudes of unemployment, of disease, of industrial accidents and disabilities, of old age, not merely freedom from destitution but freedom from want, and the enjoyment, as a right and not a favor and with no catechisms or tests, of a sufficient income to command all the essential necessaries of life." [3] It is now quite apparent that the Labor government has both the determination and the power to put the Beveridge Plan or something like it into operation. The list of countries being stirred deeply by social changes is, actually, the roll call of the nations—great and small—of the entire world. That we are living in one of the most revolutionary eras known to man is or should be an axiom of our thinking and planning for the present and future.

It is supremely important for the Christian church to acquaint itself with the needs, the dangers, and the immeasurable tragedy of the underprivileged peoples of the world. Many of its members are among them, enabling it to feel, at first hand, the despair, the anger, and the surging tide of revolt which sweeps through them. Certain general obligations are clear. The church must seek to understand their problems and help them toward an understanding couched in thoroughly realistic terms. It must seek opportunity rather than charity for them. To this end, it should seek to awaken in its privileged members a profound awareness of their, and its, especial responsibility for unbarring the barred gates of opportunity and security for the needy ones in God's family. Though the church can claim no particular ability in submitting blueprinted solutions of social, economic, and political problems, it must assert its right to keep these problems before competent men until they, under the compulsion of Christian conscience, do work out a just answer to them. It is hard to see what meaning is carried by the goal "brotherhood of man" if this task is not gladly and conscientiously accepted.

It is at this point that all such discussions of Christian responsibility in social matters tend to disappear in the mists and vagaries of an increasingly irrelevant idealism. And the reason for the disappearance is not hard to find. The actual fulfillment of the Christian hope for the common good seems to be so far beyond the reach of any realistic proposal that we find it easier to treat it as a separated rather than related reality. Yet to do this is to pervert the Christian faith from being the gospel of the salvation *of* the world to the gospel of salvation *from* the world. The church has frequently been guilty of conveying precisely that impression, and we need to be eternally on our guard against a repetition of the error today.

To this end, then, of understanding the lump which the Christian faith must leaven let us study the needs of certain large occupational groups whose present disturbances are more symptoms than causes of the deep tides of change that are moving contemporary society. I am thinking now of the special needs of the farmer, the laborer, and the businessman. Since the overwhelming majority of mankind falls into these categories, we are not working at isolated problems when we seek the spiritual implications of the grave problems which confront these groups in the modern world.

II

Mr. Herbert Agar reminds us that "Farming is not only an economic system for producing bacon and eggs; it is also a way of life." [4] It is a highly troubled and uncertain way of life today, even though it continues to engage the attention and efforts of more of mankind than any other industry. A recent careful study [5] of the political problems of Europe points out the fact that one of the permanent sources of instability and insecurity has been the uneven development and distribution of the agricultural resources of that continent. The enormous food-raising potential of Poland and the Balkan countries, for example, has been crippled both by primitive methods of farming and by the system of landownership under which, until recently, most of the land lay in large estates. [6] The enormous dislocation of populations due to war has only aggravated the problem of this region. What we see there is symptomatic of the fact that the agrarian peoples all over the world are in turmoil. Here in the United States we have not been able effectively to stem the flow of people away from farms to cities and their better-paying industries. This is particularly noticeable among the renters or tenant farmers, who find it easy to make the move. During the war the problem of farm labor was acute and unsolved. The wider problems of ownership, secure tenure, equitable prices for goods, and a higher standard of living emerged again with the end of the war.

Certain outstanding needs must be met if farming as a way of life is to regain its hold upon a sufficiently large number of persons both to produce necessary foodstuffs for our civilization and to make possible a life of dignity for the farmer. Although couched in terms which apply specifically to the American farmer, the needs to be considered obviously affect farmers the world over.

1. A greater measure of freedom due to economic security is perhaps the basic need. The farmer usually operates on limited capital. He borrows in order to plant his crops or purchase stock for feeding. Usually, he must sell the crops when harvested, regardless of price, or market the stock when the note comes due, again regardless of price. As a result quick-money crops, which deplete the soil if used too steadily, are planted. Then, too, the cost of purchase, repair, and replacement of essential implements is much higher than is usually supposed. Add to this the basic cost of the land and its improvements, and the payment of taxes, and it is obvious that farming is an extensive and expensive business enterprise. The enormous number of farms which were sold under mortgage in America between the wars is an indication of the precarious future of the farmer. It is to be noted that the collapse of farm markets and the insolvency of farming always results in a severe depression for the entire social order. Unless the very great purchasing power of the farmer and communities which depend upon him for their life can be maintained, the prosperity of industrial areas collapses forthwith. This, obviously, calls for a careful appraisal of the interdependence of the problems of the farmer and those of other occupational groups.

2. Vocational and cultural education is another of the great needs of the farmer. This is basic to any effort to raise his standard of living. Through it he can learn how to make the most efficient use of his resources—stock, land, crops, and capital funds. It will

cultivate a sense of vocation, or calling, which is an essential of dignity. It is of the essence of a vocation that it is both necessary work and appreciated as such by the rest of society. There is reason to believe that the fine work toward this end now being done in many rural areas in the United States by the 4-H clubs and other similar efforts can be extended. Such programs build in youth a sense of farming as a creative as well as secure means of living. We must not underestimate the fundamental character of this need. No amount of tinkering with markets and credits can possibly substitute for a profound appreciation of the values of rural life. There must be cultivated among our people a reverence for the earth, which God has created and empowered to bring forth fruit.[7]

3. Greater unity of action in protecting and furthering the rights of the agrarian communities is one of the most pressing needs just now. It has been recognized as a need by the farmers of our country for almost a hundred years, and various efforts have been made to meet it. But each has run head on into the innate individualism of the farmer. This is no mere fiction. It is a well-established fact, as every attempt to organize, much less regiment, the farmer can testify. As long as it is possible for him to make ends meet without sacrificing any part of his independence to the interests of common action, he will stay "on his own." His is one of the few occupations enabling a man to provide some sort of food and shelter as one of its immediate results. But today the role of the farmer is so intertwined with that of the national and international community that every session of state and national Congress considers legislation that directly affects his welfare. This fact calls for group thought and action. Fortunately, several farm groups are coming to the fore and with increasing support can provide the most numerous occupational group in the country with representation.

No field possesses greater importance for the church than the rural one. It is not overstating the matter to say that the training of ministers and missionaries equipped to help the farmers of the world toward a clearer understanding of their problems is one of the most important tasks before the church. Fortunately, a beginning has been made, and, as we grasp the issues involved, we shall throw increasing emphasis upon it.

III

Professor Arnold Toynbee says that "industrialism" and "democracy" are the two distinctive characteristics of modern civilization.[8] His study of the meaning of this for our day deserves most careful attention. He points out the grave fact that the conflict between these two factors is at the basis of the social unrest which has been shaking the Western world over the last two centuries. The needs of modern industry created huge pools of workers in cities. In its early days, industry was the personal property of one man or a few men at most. Owners were laws unto themselves in policy of purchase and sale of goods, as well as in hours, conditions, and wages of labor. Naturally enough, the ferment of democracy which overthrew the absolute monarchies of Europe one by one, placing the franchise in the hands of citizens, produced movements for greater freedom and dignity among workingmen. The labor movement, now in full swing in America, had its forerunners at an earlier day in most European countries. Various types of radical social thought and action sprang up in Germany, France, England, and Russia, to cite only the largest countries. After a long period of relative ineffectiveness, due largely to internal dissension, the labor movement became an important pivot of political power in each one. The government of Soviet Russia is known within Russia as the workingman's government. The Labor party holds undisputed power in England. An eloquent indication of the strategic power of the various labor organizations in Italy and Germany is seen in the fact that Mussolini and Hitler flattered and used them in their climb to power and liquidated them at once as soon as they arrived. Here in the United States the rising tide of self-conscious strength in labor is recognized by every political party in its platform and other public appeals. It is safe to say that wherever industrialism and democracy are factors in the life of a people the workers will become an increasingly influential, if not dominant, factor in government.

Obviously, these labor movements must be regarded as efforts to meet deep-lying needs in the life of working people. What are those needs?

1. *"Common justice"* is a cover-all phrase, to be sure, but it does indicate a number of very concrete needs. It refers to stable and adequate incomes, to insurance against the hazards of illness and accident, to assurance of care in age. It means an end to the idea and practice of paternalism as an acceptable relationship between employer and employee. It means the practice of the now legally established right of collective bargaining on all matters pertaining to the vital interests of the worker. It means equality of franchise and the end of discrimination in employment based upon race or religion. It means that antilabor laws shall be removed from the books and that the cause of labor shall be given a fair hearing in cases of dispute. It means, to use the incisive words of the National Study Conference on the Churches and a Just and Durable Peace:

1. That every man should have the opportunity to share in the ownership of both personal and productive property, such as a home, a farm and economic enterprises.
2. That every member and family of the human race have a right to steady employment and to earn an income such as may provide the necessities of life and growth and is in accord with the wealth-producing capacity of their day and the requirements of responsible conservation of natural resources.
3. That in early years every individual has the right to full-time educational opportunities with reasonable consideration of his talents, interests, and probable vocation; that in later years every individual is entitled to economic security in retirement and the continuation of cultural opportunities; that in the whole span of life every individual is entitled to adequate health service and professional medical care; and that in the productive years there is the universal obligation to work in some socially necessary service.
4. That every man has the right to employment of a kind that is consistent with human dignity and self-respect, and to such leisure as is essential for cultural and spiritual development; that employers of all kinds should recognize and safeguard these rights.[9]

2. *Unity among workers* in facing their special problems is an essential step toward meeting them. Wherever the person and rights of the worker, his family, and his fellows are involved in a problem or situation, the worker must exercise the right to speak not alone as an individual but even more decisively through a group voice. No employer, however benevolent his intentions, should desire to assume the responsibility of speaking for the workingman on such matters. When employers do make this attempt, both the worker and the conscience of the community must be prepared to resist them. Only when the worker's right to speak for himself is widely recognized and respected can the processes of democracy be said to be at work in industry. We are better able to appreciate the necessity of effective labor unions when we study the vicious exploitations of workers which occur where they have no corporate voice. It is hard for us to visualize the evils attendant upon the wholesale importation of unskilled Chinese workers to operate the tin mines and of Indians to work the rubber plantations of Malaya. Throughout the Orient there is only the feeble beginning of an effective labor movement. In Africa even the beginnings have not yet been made. That it will grow in power as industrialism increases is both axiomatic and hopeful. It is putting the matter mildly to say that without unity among working people in contemporary society there is little use in talking of the derivative virtues of dignity and freedom.

The church can not presume to say what form this unity of action among workers shall take. No known form can be freed from the dangers which beset any democratic structure, namely, seizure of power by one or a few leaders, worker-centered actions which minimize the rights of the employer and the general public, intimidation of nonunion workers by the union, development of political pressure out of proportion to the number of citizens constituting the labor union. Real as such dangers are, they must nonetheless be incurred both because working people have so frequently seen other groups use them to labor's disadvantage and because they represent the inevitable possibility of evil use which is inseparable from any kind of social power. The worker's use of the power accruing from the exercise of his democratic rights will be disciplined by his sense of responsibility and community in the social whole—which must be reckoned among his needs.

3. *A sense of community* with the whole of society is a basic need if the growing power of labor is to remain a socially creative factor. Of course, labor is not alone in needing this outreach. Any social group—whether farmer, labor union, National Association of Manufacturers, or church—without an awareness of its obligations to the rest of society is bound to be a menace, first to others, then to itself.

Every problem which labor faces is faced from another angle by another group—employer, stockholder, competitor, and consumer. Every decision which labor makes alters all such perspectives. It follows, then, that the wisest decisions, in the long run, will be those made in the light of awareness of the total problem. Labor, as well as other interested groups, is expected to be concerned about its own rights in the matter—this is its obligation both to itself and to the public—but it, and other groups, must cultivate a keener appreciation of the rights of others likewise involved in the issue.

It is not to be supposed that working people will achieve this sense of world community any more readily than any other group. They will need to turn a deaf ear to the voice of nationalism with its dangerous counsels of economic isolationism or economic imperialism. Accustomed, through tragic experience, to bitter struggles for their own rights, they must learn to see their problems in the light of the common good. To put the matter positively, the worker, like the industrialist, will want to work as hard and as eagerly to maintain world peace as he worked to win the war. The struggle for a just world order is lost for good and all unless the rank and file of mankind is prepared to accept the sacrificial discipline which must undergird an enduring peace.

At this point the Christian church can make a unique contribution to the workers of the world. Its affirmation, "We believe that

God is Father of all peoples and races, Jesus Christ is His Son, that we and all men are brothers, and that man is of infinite worth as a child of God," [10] lays an enduring foundation for world comity. Not only is the quality of dignity vouchsafed the person, but the added quality of community is likewise indicated as a social necessity and possibility. Wherever the Christian gospel becomes a steadily deepening part of the life of a people, the possibility of a stable, just world order is enlarged to that extent. It is the task of the church to confront workers with this vision of the oneness of all men in God and ask them to use it as the frame of reference in their plans and policies on social questions.

IV

Let us consider now the businessman. By "businessman" we mean anyone who is engaged in the manufacture, purchase, or sale of goods. It is a broad category, including the great industrialist as well as the owner of the corner store. The latter is engaged in a comparatively simple business enterprise consisting almost wholly of the purchase and sale of a limited number of articles. Back of him stand the producer, wholesaler, and banker, furnishing him the needed goods and capital. Confronting him are a relatively few consumers with whom he is personally acquainted and to whom he is strictly accountable for the quality and price of his goods and the ethics of his business practices. But he and the powerful industrialist differ in degree, not in kind, so far as their general occupation is concerned.

The industrialist is engaged in the manufacture as well as the sale of goods. He must have raw materials, plants, workers, marketing and sales, and consumers in order to keep his business going. The hub of his enterprise is the capital with which to run it. He must have money for purchase, buildings, tools, replacements, wages, and marketing. He must show a profit by declaring dividends on invested stock in order to keep sufficient capital at hand for conducting the business. But the business is more than the capital at work in it. It is the entire network of all activities essential to the production or purchase and sale of goods. The businessman, strictly speaking, is the one who, through the control of capital, controls the initiative in the business.

Historically, the businessman in the Western industrialized world has depended upon three factors for the solvency and growth of his business: capital, competition, and freedom of control in policy. The need for capital in business is obvious. Competition has been regarded as producing initiative, invention, and growth both in quantity and quality of goods. It has also been regarded as the consumer's guarantee of high-quality merchandise at the lowest possible price. Freedom of control in policy has been stressed with emphasis varying all the way from "Let the purchaser beware"—or no controls except those imposed by the businessman himself—to "Let the public good be served"—or strict supervision by government as representative of the people to safeguard their welfare.

The businessman today is seriously worried about certain widespread developments in all three of these historically accepted factors in the health of business. Developments in tax policies have aimed at the strict limitation of the accumulation of capital. Developments of monopolies of various sorts have drastically curtailed the anticipated benefits of competition. Freedom of control in policy is now modified by both governmental regulations and the rising insistence of the workers that they are entitled to be heard on such matters. The gravity of these developments, from the viewpoint of business traditionally conceived, can hardly be overstated. They actually forecast new social systems of one kind or another, whether state collectivism, or communism, or one in which the production and sale of goods is taken under the wing of consumers in some type of co-operative. The majority of businessmen, frightened by these possibilities, are begging for the return to "free enterprise," which, presumably, means greater freedom from governmental regulations and various monopolistic practices within business. A few seem to advocate a return to ruthless, socially irresponsible capitalism in which the measure of the excellence of a business is the size of profit it shows without regard to the means by which the profit is made or the use to which it shall be put.

By virtue of the fact that the Christian church, in the immediate future, will have its centers of greatest strength both in numbers and in freedom of expression and action in our Western, industrial society, she must consider these problems of the businessman as being as truly hers as are those of the farmer and worker. She has not fulfilled her mission by occasional prophetic denunciations of unethical, un-Christian business practices and principles, however valuable and necessary such expressions are when true. She must seek to Christianize the conscience of the businessmen in her fellowship until they consider their problems in the new perspective of the good of the common man.

The needs of the businessman are not different in principle from those of the worker. This fact, as well as any other, attests the organic character of business as such. Like the worker, the businessman needs common justice, unity with his fellow businessmen, and a sense of community with the social whole. A slightly different phrasing of these needs may facilitate a clearer statement of the specific needs of the businessman.

The businessmen of the United States have kept the public well informed as to what they think their needs are. Their national conventions and associations have drawn up one platform after another of basic needs and goals of business. The reason behind this energetic output of ideas is not hard to find: the businessman thinks it is a little too much to be demoted from messiah to whipping boy in one generation! Only yesterday he was looked upon as the great hope of a new world of plenty for all men. Now he is widely regarded as the one whose principles and practices have proved to be the evil genius within our social order. No one knows better than a thoughtful businessman that both extremes are grossly untrue. He is interested in understanding his role in society and in interpreting it to others. Underlying his various statements of goals are certain basic needs which deserve attention.

1. The businessman needs *a sense of freedom* in his work. Dig-

nity and justice lose all meaning for him if this is denied. By freedom we do not mean a condition of ethical and social irresponsibility. Few businessmen want this. The businessman, like the farmer and the worker, needs certain large areas in which the responsibility of choice and initiative lies with him. This right belongs to him because he is a man rather than because he owns the capital which controls the enterprise. No democratically inclined society will neglect this need. It has not yet been demonstrated that any form of collectivism, whether state socialism or communism, does actually make adequate allowance for it. So long as we cherish the dignity and depend upon the choices of the individual citizen, we must grant and safeguard the fact of freedom to all citizens.

2. The businessman needs to accept *the public good* as the basic criterion of what he does. Naturally, this couples *freedom* with *social responsibility* in a thoroughly wholesome way. The socially corporate character of business will not admit of any other criterion. Many persons and many interests are as acutely and deeply involved in any business enterprise as are those who own the capital or constitute the board of directors of the business. In other words, a business is a kind of community operating within the social whole, either for the good or for the ill of that whole. In a democratic society a way should be found for an actual sharing of control, privilege, and responsibility. This process should begin within the business itself, linking worker and owner in some form of democratic management. Nor can the process of democratic control be arrested at that point since the larger part of the public lies beyond worker and owner and is entitled to have its welfare protected. This, obviously, is the province of government. As Lincoln wisely said, "The legitimate object of government is to do for a community of people whatever they need to have done but cannot do at all; or cannot so well do, for themselves, in their separate and individual capacities. In all that the people can individually do as well for themselves, government ought not to interfere."

This observation suggests the limits which must be observed in the debate as to the role of government in business. If business under the banner of free enterprise can solve, not alone the problems of the production, purchase, and sale of goods, but also the related problems of exploitation of natural and human resources, unemployment, and social security for all, there would be no call or need for government to assume the initiative in such matters. On the basis of our experience in the recent past, there is reason to believe that these problems are of such magnitude that neither business nor government alone can solve them. The public good requires that they be met under the prevailing social system, if possible, but, that failing, under another system. The fact that no perfect system has as yet been hit upon cannot be expected to preclude experimentation that will vary in revolutionary character in direct proportion to the intensity of existing social needs.

3. The businessman needs *a consciousness of the world community*. He is already well aware of the interrelatedness of the world so far as business is concerned. But he, like the farmer and the worker, tends to do his thinking in nationalistic or empire terms. It is precisely this limitation of the field of primary responsibility that must be challenged by the church, not alone in behalf of the gospel, but also in behalf of her own interests and those of the nation as well. We are slow to face up to the implications of the fact that war and peace, prosperity and depression are equally indivisible. We cannot permanently protect our own interests at the expense of those of other nations and peoples. It is one thing—and good—to assist industrially and culturally backward portions of the world toward a higher level of development of their trade potential and cultural life. But it is quite another thing to regard them and the riches of their region as fair prey for wealthier, more powerful peoples. The day of economic exploitation of the world's undeveloped resources and of the political and cultural domination of large portions of mankind by a few aggressive peoples is over, and, for the good of all members of the world community, this fact must be recognized.

It would be unfair to single out the businessman of yesterday as the object of special condemnation in this matter. He was loudly applauded by his fellow-citizens, especially those whose income was dependent upon the success of his ventures. But the fact that the power to initiate these enterprises and, to a large measure, to determine their moral character rested with him, places upon him a special responsibility for the injustices, as well as the more favorable consequences, that have ensued.

Business, of itself, cannot and will not plan for a world community. It will share in whatever notion of world order dominates the people among whom it has its base. It is the task of the Christian church to communicate its vision of a world community to the businessmen of the Western, industrial world and stimulate them to accept the common good of the common man everywhere as the rock-bottom fact in their plans for the future.

V

Whoever thinks such great problems are not the immediate concern of the Christian church is urged to read and reread the Parable of the Last Judgment (Matthew 25:31-46) until its single, searching meaning converts his soul. If we as churchmen feel we cannot concern ourselves with the problems that harass our people, we are declaring the irrelevance of the gospel to the very issues that are crippling and killing men.

Every great church now has a "social creed." Twenty-five years ago this was a novelty, now it is a commonplace—almost too much so! And the end of the social awakening of the church is not yet. All churches are centering attention upon the rural life problem. The Roman Catholic Church is conducting training schools for labor leaders. The Methodist Church has begun the appointment of men as "chaplains" to organized labor. The National Association of Manufacturers has sponsored a nation-wide series of conferences between businessmen and clergy, hoping to iron out some of the misunderstandings between them. A representative of organized labor is an accredited member of the Federal Council's Commission on World Order. During the recent industrial strife committees of clergymen repeatedly interceded in the name of common justice and the public welfare.

Efforts like these can and must be multiplied a thousandfold in these perilous times.

In February, 1947, the Federal Council of the Churches of Christ in America convened a National Study Conference on the Church and Economic Life—the first but not the last of its kind. Recognizing that "The Church cannot provide blueprints" the conference asserted that, "It can give perspectives"—and must do so on all basic economic problems. It called for a careful training of Christian clergy and laity alike in the understanding of economic problems. So far from being a wholly new venture, Professor A. T. Mollegan has recently published a brief account of the "Historical Development of the Christian Testimony Concerning Economic Relations." [11] He finds social concern imbedded in and inseparable from the fact of community. Those who rejoice in the church's determination to champion the common man have the added confidence of knowing that they are the lineal descendants of the prophets of ancient Israel.

All this may seem like a far cry from "the simple gospel" which the church exists to proclaim, but, as a matter of cold fact, it is inseparable from it. Ernest Troeltsch saw this and wrote, "The more clearly . . . that the Churches have discerned the fact that all higher spiritual culture is largely dependent upon the economic basis of life, the more earnestly they have thrown their energies into an endeavor to understand and solve these questions." [12] The only known way to preach the good news to all men is to so relate it to the deepest needs of their life and day that they will see in and through it their way to a new day. That is why the church will be the champion of "the common man" as he works his way into a century of the common good.

Chapter VII ✦ RELIGIOUS FAITH UNDERGIRDS DEMOCRACY

I

If it is true that misery loves company, then religion and democracy ought to be seeing a good deal of each other these days; both are decidedly on the defensive in the modern world. Religion has been having a hard fight of it with one foe or another over the last two hundred years. But the testing days of democracy as a form of government, a kind of culture and society, are of more recent date, beginning in dead earnest in 1917 with the Russian Revolution. During the intervening years it has become an epithet for an increasing number of nations all over the world. The recent war was presented to the peoples of the world as a struggle for the democratic way of life against the forces of tyranny. Our own President, the late Franklin D. Roosevelt, tried to tell us that "religion and democracy stand or fall together." That, as every student of history knows, is a misstatement of the actual relationship between them. Now that the war is over, democracy continues to be well spoken of in some countries that have not the slightest interest in its historic meaning and forms. Most of us think in terms of Russia, Franco's Spain, and Tito's Yugoslavia when we think this way. But Dr. Paul Hutchinson in his *The New Leviathan* brings in a gloomy report about the anti-democratic trend plainly discernible in the life of our own nation. The forces of state collectivism are gaining headway in many important fields, he says, and we are likely to witness the severe curtailment of democracy unless faith in it can be rejuvenated and many of its basic practices and relationships be restored.

Believing as I profoundly do both in the Christian religion as the true view of life and in democracy as that form of society best fitted for the Christian view to mature in, I am concerned to discover those points at which Christianity can contribute something essential to the survival of democracy. For, I am convinced, the paramount social problem before us today is this: *Can democracy survive?* What I want to know is this: Can Christianity help democracy meet the challenge of skepticism as to the validity of the democratic ideal? Can Christianity furnish the fertile soil of positive faith in man, in history, and in the future which is essential to the survival of man's confidence in democracy? Can Christianity help keep democracy from becoming a dogma, a static entity; help keep it face forward, growing in terms of new problems? Can Christianity lift democracy above the provincialism of nationalism and the barbarism of imperialism, thus enabling it to be the champion of human rights wherever these are imperiled or denied?

These serious and searching questions deserve more time and much more wisdom than we can hope to bring to bear upon them, but they are too momentous to be ignored. A wrong answer is better than no answer since it manifests an awareness of the importance of the question and a determination to get an answer to it.

II

The first question we face can be stated in simple terms: Are men capable of democracy? We are not asking whether we want democracy or whether we are willing to work for it. We are raising the much deeper question as to whether there is any use even trying to achieve it. We shall find that uncertainty on this basic problem has been found wherever men have tried to think their way into the meaning of democracy.

A good working definition of democracy is Lincoln's famous phrase, "a government of the people, by the people, and for the people." But this conception is widely challenged both in theory and practice. That gifted snob, Henry Adams, in his *Degeneration of the Democratic Dogma* wrote, "Democracy is an infinite mass of conflicting minds and conflicting interests which . . . becomes resolved into . . . a vapor, which loses in collective intellectual energy in proportion to the perfection of its expansion." This is another way of saying that the farther you spread democracy, the less actual interest in it and understanding of it there is among people in general. A militant minority can agitate for and finally win democratic rights for the majority, but the majority will let them slip through negligent fingers. That may be what prompted Carlyle to say, "Democracy is a plurality of blockheads."

Lincoln's conception of democracy has had hard sledding in history. To begin with, it has seldom been tried and when it has the results have not been encouraging. Democracy in Periclean Greece lived with a measure of effectiveness for one hundred years, but it weakened and finally fell. It failed because it was unable to manage the vices that arose within it. It was irremediably weakened by internal enemies before it succumbed to external ones.

As the story unfolds in Dr. Will Durant's *The Life of Greece*,[1] it is given the fitting title, "The Suicide of Greece." A spirit of profound provincialism pervaded the city-states; it was each one for itself with little or no thought for a common good. They lost all notion, if they ever had it, that they were bound together in a common historic destiny. Greed for goods and lust for power pushed the stronger cities, notably Athens and Sparta, in the direction of empire. Prosperity brought moral corruption and spiritual decadence, as it always does. Rivalry between the most powerful states was inevitable, and soon the forces of Athens and Sparta were opening the veins of one of the richest civilizations ever to grace this earth. It is impossible to improve upon Dr. Durant's terse summary, "The death of Greek democracy was both a violent and a natural death, in which the fatal agents were the organic disorders of the system; the sword of Macedon merely added the final blow." [2]

Unfortunately, democracy seems to be in a similar predicament today. After having been in operation to some extent in the

Western world for several hundred years, it is now fighting for its very life against doubts and vices within and deadly foes without. Why is this? you want to know. Why is it that democracy has so much trouble if it is based upon a true appraisal of human capacities? One of the few philosopher-statesmen of our day, Professor T. V. Smith of the University of Chicago laid bare the heart of the democratic problem in this penetrating observation, "That men will live for private gain we know; that they will die for public ends we know; but whether average men in the continuous long run will work efficiently for public ends we do not know." [3] Nor is Dr. Smith alone in this doubt. Some of the most disciplined minds the human race has ever produced are sure that you cannot count on the average man's willingness to do those things that are essential to democracy. You cannot count upon his own personal long-time interest in the public good; you cannot count upon his being willing to sacrifice his own ease and convenience in the long run for the achievement of the public good.

Plato, who lived two hundred years after the golden age of democracy in Greece, seeing with his own eyes the decadence of democracy, brings in a most challenging indictment of democracy as a form of government. He saw the crumbling democracy of his day put his beloved teacher, Socrates, to death, and he never forgave it that crime. To him, democracy is always and inevitably corrupted by human greed and pride. And the reason is simple: *Democracy gives the individual more freedom than he can manage.* When you give an individual freedom, what does he do? Does he ask, What is the public good? What ought to be done in behalf of the general welfare? He does not! He does what he wants done—with the emphasis falling decidedly upon "what he wants done." He alone is the determiner of what he wants. He is primarily concerned with his own welfare, assuming that others are similarly concerned and that as each man gets what he wants all will be satisfied. When conflict arises, as it inevitably does, each individual is quite willing to impose upon the rights of another in order to secure his own. No, says Plato, you cannot count on the average man's interest in the democratic ideal. You will find that he will utilize the freedom democracy gives him to gratify his own selfish and uncriticized desires. He will regard it as an opportunity to exploit his own undisciplined passions at the expense of other people and their freedom.

Democracy breaks up as a result of internal changes, the Platonic indictment continues. The breakup proceeds according to a more or less regular pattern. Many men see one man gain an increasing amount of power. They want to share in its fruits so they gravitate to him and ask him to be their protector. Soon you have a number of such leaders or focal points of power and a clash between them makes civil war inevitable. The victor in this strife will make brash promises to win and hold the allegiance of all the people. He will promise them bread and circuses or anything else that they appear to want if only they will consign to him their right to make the decisions by which they are to live. And people will do just that, Plato exclaims. You are living in a fool's paradise if you think you can count on the average man to be concerned about public welfare. Try it, and you simply move from a short-lived experience of individual freedom to a long-lived experience of tyranny.

Plato has powerful support in this position. All monarchists, absolutists, and totalitarians share his distrust of democracy. Machiavelli [4] and Hobbes,[5] two of Europe's most influential political thinkers, would agree with him. Plato sought his solution in *The Philosopher King;* Machiavelli in the all-powerful *The Prince;* Hobbes in *The Omnicompetent State.*

III

Who, then, does believe that man is capable of democracy? As I understand the situation, there are two groups of thinkers— one secular, the other religious—who have some confidence in the democratic potential in people. A secularist is one who does not believe religion has anything of very great significance to offer toward solving this problem of the weakness of human nature. He believes we may be able to develop a civilization on the minimum basis of "live and let live." He argues that possibly, with this beginning, we may be able to build up a civilization over a period of several hundred years in which we can learn to respect each other's rights. Not because we love each other! Not at all! But because we will learn the hard lesson that this is the law of survival: I shall learn to respect your rights not because I like you but because I want you to learn to respect mine. The secularist says we can build a powerful social ethic on this basis, the ethic of "one for all and all for one." No matter how selfish an individual is, he will learn to recognize the fact that he is bound up with the group and must live with that group in such a way as to enable it to survive if he is to survive. But his basic interest in so doing is in himself, not in the group. Since he is interested in himself and the conditions of his own survival, he will curb his own desires, greed, and prejudice. Naturally, being human, he will cherish them as long and as much as he can safely do. He will continue to be a decided individual but will be willing to recognize the fact that his individuality must combine somehow or other with the social welfare.

All of this looks plausible enough, but it suffers from a fatal weakness. It overlooks what our fathers called "the gravity of sin," the profound weakness, the "depravity" of human nature. We must begin our thinking about man and his capabilities with the grim facts of greed, passion, and prejudice. We do not begin with greed, for example, as a fact to be found and faced in the future; we begin with it as a fact now, as an active factor in our daily living and thinking. We do not consciously will and choose to be prejudiced; we begin our conscious life by being prejudiced. We do not suddenly come to a stage of maturity, look about us, and say we are against this or that minority group for this or that reason. From earliest infancy we breathe in the prejudices which mold the patterns of our mature mind. There is no point at which we begin consciously to be prejudiced against the Negro, for example. There is, however, a point in our life when we consciously recognize that prejudice for the blight that it is. Why do we cherish it? Why do we not cry with Tennyson:

> Am I mad that I should cherish
> That which bears but bitter fruit?
> I will pluck it from my bosom
> Though my heart be at the root! [6]

We cherish this prejudice because it ministers to our desire for status, esteem, honor, and privilege. We like to regard persons as less than we are because we thus feel greater than we actually are. We like to have people weaker than we are because we feel stronger than we actually are. We like to have people work for us and serve us because it gives us an illusion of pride and mastery. Therefore, we continue feeding prejudice because it ministers to that rapacious self-esteem called pride which knows that it cannot stand up to the criticism of reason and conscience.

These, then—pride, greed, prejudice, ignorance—are the basic spiritual problems of democracy. They will not be solved simply by overthrowing this or that political and military power which challenges us at any given moment, however dangerous the challenge may be. No matter how many external enemies we conquer, these basic problems will persist. Is it going to be possible for us to grapple effectively with these challenges directed at the heart of democracy? If not, every attempt at democracy will die in the throes of a revolution which leads to tyranny.

I am convinced that the Christian religion has the courage to look at these basic problems squarely, and having looked at them, can retain faith in God and man. Nonreligious democrats say: "Give us time; these problems will work themselves out." But they did not work themselves out in any previous civilization, and they had hundreds of years in which to do it! All such civilizations went down pleading for the time they did not have. They, too, thought that somehow or other their problems would solve themselves if only given enough time. Problems like these never solve themselves. They but grow worse if time is the only unguent applied. Even so, the sands of time have about run out in the hourglass of our civilization.

The Christian religion has a long-time acquaintance with these spiritual problems of greed, pride, prejudice, and selfish individualism; in fact, they form the factual basis for the theological doctrine of human depravity, of original sin. From long and bitter experience, the Christian faith knows that a man must struggle from the very beginning of his life against this grim and forbidding heritage. So far from stopping with the doctrine of original sin, the Christian faith announces the doctrine of the grace of God! It says in no uncertain terms that these sins can be conquered, conquered by faith in a God of love whose love is strong enough to overcome any evil, and a God near to each man. The individual can submit to God's will so completely that his reason and conscience will be able to curb and control, even though they can never eradicate, this tendency toward greed, pride, and prejudice. Human reason and conscience are, therefore, the gifts of God to man, gifts whereby we can think His thoughts after Him, whereby we seek to order our life after His will for us. Such gifts remind us that it is never wholly accurate to say, "God *has* spoken." The truth of the matter is that God not only has spoken but continues to speak to those who are willing to hear. The fact of God is the bedrock upon which the Christian faith bases its triumphant confidence in man and in the future.

Professor Urban of Yale once said, "For some generations now man has been trying to decide whether he is merely a high-grade simian or a Son of God." Though evidence mounts to the contrary, the Christian religion continues to believe that we are sons of God. But, as our own sons can leave our homes even against our will, so we can leave the family of God, can forsake the meaning of sonship to Him. That does not mean that God forsakes us; He will follow us wherever we are and go, seeking to win us again into that relationship of love. The Christian religion confronts us with the choice—simian or son of God. But we must make it. Once we submit our mind and will to the will of God as we see it in Jesus Christ, we gain a sense of direction and we slowly win the strength to move away from that kind of degradation of life which these perennial evils that threaten human nature always bring.

The Christian confronts the question, "Are we capable of democracy?" with the answer, "With God's help, yes. We are capable of fashioning a society of the people, by the people, and for the people which shall not perish from this earth. It is possible for us, by means of reason and conscience under the guidance of God, to live our life in such a way that we can learn to love each other, can learn to live together as a family, recognizing the fact that another has a claim upon our concern and cooperation not simply as a citizen but as a brother in Christ."

IV

There is another important matter on which religion can bring real aid and comfort to the embattled democratic ideal. And that is on the tremendous problem of social change. Professor Arnold Toynbee gives as his first reason for the decay and disintegration of civilization "the intractability of institutions." It is a fact, of course, that established institutions are characterized by a blind resistance to change. They become complacent, i.e., at peace with themselves. They become self-satisfied and self-perpetuating. They magnify their virtues and minimize their vices. They trumpet their achievements to the heavens but "mum's the word" about their shortcomings. They seek "good men," "safe men" for positions of leadership, men who can be trusted, can be counted on to give the applecart a gentle ride. They reserve their choicest epithets for anyone who demands a drastic change in affairs. He is an agitator, a troublemaker, a rabble rouser, an anarchist. He will be called a socialist or a communist or a fascist depending upon which way the international winds happen to be blowing at the moment.

The older an institution gets the more it is tempted to define itself in terms of its past instead of its present and future. It invokes its Founding Fathers or its Spiritual Forebears whenever trouble threatens. Let a storm arise and it will seek to stretch the mantle of their thought and faith over the centuries until it covers their heads. And it will persist even though the mantle be torn beyond recognition in the effort! The persistent ailment of institutions calls to mind Luther's famous story of the colloquy between God and the devil. God said, "I have a great idea that will overcome you!" "I'm not afraid of it," the devil replied, "I'll institutionalize it!"

Why is it institutions behave this way once they become established? Is their "intractability" as inevitable as it is fatal?

While no one can be sure of having the whole truth about so complex a matter, two reasons do deserve a hearing. One calls attention to the fact that man is afraid of the future. On the whole, he would rather endure the ills he has than fly to others he knows not of. Consequently, even those who suffer injustice under the established institution would rather continue under it than risk worse under something else. Until, of course, like the peasants in the French Revolution, their agony becomes unendurable; then the deluge comes. The other reason grows out of the fact that privileged groups tend to freeze the *status quo* at the point of their maximum privilege. Political machines, whether in the cities of the North or the southern states, are excellent examples of privileged groups in politics. They vigorously resist all changes that they cannot turn to their own immediate political advantage. They control elections, by foul means more frequently than fair; they seek to defame rather than answer critics of their policy. Although they know all of the catchwords of democracy, its spirit is far from them.

Yet change must and will come. We have no choice in that matter. People will not starve quietly in a world of actual and potential plenty. They will not forever bear patiently indignities and inequities based upon race. They will not endure endlessly domination by another people. Change will come, must come— let us never forget that! It can be by evolution but, that failing, it will be by revolution.

The Christian faith has real assistance to offer the democratic ideal at this point. For Christians of all people ought to be prepared to face the fact that changes must come; they ought to be ready to lead in the search for the proper form the change should take. As a matter of fact, a vital Christian faith will inaugurate many fundamental social changes because it cannot rest content with the social order in which we live.

Jesus felt that all vital religion is a leaven which keeps working until "it leaveneth the whole lump." It takes time. Its work is never done. The leaven of the Christian faith is its conviction about God, Christ, and the good life. It begins with the reality and centrality of God in life and in the universe. It moves from this to the position that we have our clearest revelation of His will for men in the life and teachings of Jesus Christ. It concludes by emphasizing the possibility of the good life as one in which the God-given rights of personal dignity, worth, and freedom develop in terms of social privilege and responsibility.

Put ideas like these in life and they are sure to act as leaven. They have brought about some of the most significant developments imaginable. Consider how the lot of the slave, the peasant, and the laboring man in the Graeco-Roman world in the second century, for example, was made easier by the leaven of the Christian religion. For whenever one of these persons in the downtrodden classes of that day became a Christian, he immediately ceased to be a slave in spirit; he stepped into a fellowship which accepted him as a brother in Christ and an equal before God. This was a status no slave, working man, or peasant in the Graeco-Roman world had ever dreamed possible. Here came the Christian religion, like light into darkness, proclaiming that he was that sort of person, entitled to live in that sort of fellowship. Nor was it simply a verbal reward. When he became a member of that warm persuasive fellowship, it easily meant more than any other relationship. It opened his days with a meeting for song and prayer; it closed with a common meal out of which our communion service has grown. It surrounded his days with a kind of spiritual ministration, making sacraments of them. The Christian religion said to the underprivileged, the dispossessed man of the ancient world, "You have an immortal soul worth more than your body will ever be worth. See to it your immortal soul is safely kept in God's control. You have nothing to fear from what man can do to you in this life."

That sort of approach obviously would not result in a head-on assault on the institution of slavery during that day, and it did not. But the doom of slavery was pronounced by the Christian religion when the ideal of brotherhood was sown as a seed in Christian ethics, for slavery and brotherhood have nothing, finally, in common. Serfdom and brotherhood have nothing, finally, in common. There is no place in the Christian conception of brotherhood for underprivileged and dispossessed men and women, whether individuals or races. There is no way you can so pervert the Christian ethic as to sanction the kinds of discrimination which somehow or other have been clung to jealously by men and women, even in the name of Christ, through many years and centuries. When the seeds of brotherhood are sown in a social order, they are perennials that will keep right on pushing up the plants of justice and equity until underprivilege and dispossession cease to be characteristics of that society.

The Christian emphasis upon charity is another example of the leaven working in the lump. The early Christians said to the poor and needy, "You are one of us and we of you. We will share our goods with you and do everything else in our power to minister to your needs." This emphasis led, over a long period of years, to the development of hospitals, to the encouragement of medical science, to a turning of the minds of Christian men and women to their responsibility for meeting a need. Naturally, this was not an even development proceeding with escalator-like regularity. There were fits and starts; in one generation great progress would be made, only to be lost in the next. But the direction of the development was never in doubt. It is no accident that the very word "hospital" grows out of the word "hospice," which originally meant a place where men could come for rest, care, and refreshment. Nor is it an accident that one of the first great medical centers of Europe, the University of Padua, grew up under the control of the Christian church. The intelligent and highly skilled forms of social service we use today grew out of the careful nurturing of the humanitarian will-to-help which through the centuries has been and is an inseparable part of the Christian religion.

As long as we keep on emphasizing the idea that all men are sons of God and equal in the sight of God—just so long as Christian churches keep on saying and believing that—we shall be making progress toward changing the social institutions of our day. It may be that the only progress we are able to discern in any given age is this: *Our institutions will be brought under the judgment of that insight.* But that is a prerequisite of progress; for an institution must be seen to be failing, to be inadequate, before men will try to change it fundamentally.

Looking over Christian history, then, we ought to be prepared to face the plain fact that changes must come. They have come and they will continue to come in our social order, for the Christian religion can never rest content with the social order in which we live. It probes our way of life with a keen, razor-edged ethic that brings under the judgment of God's will and love not only our own personal lives and sins but also our institutions—family, school, church, government, economic order. Under the leading of that ethic only one question is open to us as Christian men and women: How shall the needed changes be brought about? All that we are or hope to be, all that we hold dear, all that we have found good must continue to grow "in the Grace of God unto perfection."

V

Christianity's agitation for social change is a real factor in our own day. I wish time permitted me to submit a careful summary of the many important conferences held in various parts of the world by Christian churches over the last ten years. Laymen and ministers alike participated in them, seeking to understand the basic problems of our day and the church's relationship to them. The conferences have been held all over the world, in Asia, Europe, and America. Representatives of nearly all Christian churches were in them, in either official or unofficial capacity. The conference that met at Madras, India, in 1938, heard the challenge: *There must be a new order for the world. That order must be the Kingdom of God. Changes must come. The churches must face and help the acute needs of man. The Christian conscience must be awakened. Christian solutions must be sought!* [7]

Those who met at Malvern in 1941 heard an angry layman speak some very searching words. Sir Richard Acland said to the assembled churchmen:

For over one hundred and fifty years you have neglected your duty . . . because of sheer funk. . . . The whole structure of society . . . is, from the Christian point of view, rotten and must permanently frustrate your efforts to create for the individual the possibility of a Christian life. . . . This has given Hitler the opportunity for saying, "To hell with the whole order." . . . He said this, and from despairing humanity he wrung forth a tremendous and dynamic response. . . . In order to save humanity from the horror of . . . Naziism, we must find a way of living superior, not merely to Nazism, but to that which we ourselves knew before. . . . We are unprepared for this. . . . You must be prepared to offend people who are determined to preserve the existing order. . . . I beg of you now to proclaim the new society openly. . . . So only will you save yourselves and us.[8]

I might say that it represents many a preacher's dream of paradise when laymen speak words like that!

From the National Study Conference of the Federal Council, held in Cleveland, Ohio, January, 1945, came this spiritual ultimatum:

The church must . . . condemn any failure of our economic system to meet the basic needs which have been indicated. We must ask our people to recognize that in order to supply these needs for all, many changes may be necessary in our economic practices. These changes will probably lie in the direction of a larger measure of social planning and control than characterized our pre-war system. They should be brought about by democratic processes and should be consistent with Christian principles with respect to the worth of personality and the value of freedom. We should not allow our devotion to any single system or method to deny to anyone the basic requirements for "the Good Life". . . . In order to maintain our democracy at a high level it must continually be adjusted to meet the necessities of history and the demands of justice. Only if our domestic order is born again with fresh vision and determination to meet the needs of men can America fulfill her new mission and bring hope and encouragement to a broken world.[9]

The only question is whether Christian citizens are going to ask for and receive the full measure of the tremendous responsibility outlined in this challenge. Other forms of government may urge their citizens to trust the matter to them. But no democracy can or will make such a request. To relieve us of personal responsibility in the matter of the moral values of our country's policy and leadership is to relieve us of our Christian ethic as well as our citizenship, and we propose to lose neither.

Democracy should be more hospitable to all thrusts toward profound change than any other form of society. For like religion, democracy's job is never done. A society of, by, and for the people will always be imperfectly realized on this earth. The enemies of this ideal society are ignorance, inherited wrong, and entrenched privilege. They must be mastered in and by each generation. Those who have power are going to neither give it up easily nor acquiesce graciously in public surveillance of the way they use it. We have no choice but to challenge these ancient enemies of the democratic ideal at every turn, in and through the schools and the government and, above all, through an intelligent and socially-minded church. Religion and democracy can walk hand in hand as we seek to bring into existence here in America a democratic government. But notice must be served on lovers of democracy that, in America at least, the direction and driving power for change must come from the ethical ideals of the Jewish-Christian tradition if religion is to be a collaborator in the change. This rules out appeals to class hate and race prejudice as motives for change. And it is high time that such were ruled out! Rational, purposive change is the law of life for democracy and religion alike. Democracy must be guarded against the nemesis of social order; it must not be permitted to harden into an unyielding dogma. No group of Americans, however prominent, can be permitted to define democracy in terms of their own welfare.

To speak thus is not to depreciate the democracy which we have; rather it is to arouse it to its present task. The permanent problem of democracy—one that no previous democracy solved —is how to keep on growing in terms of fundamental problems. Notable steps have been taken in the past; for example, democracy outgrew the duel and vigilante law. Few thoughtful citizens now doubt the wisdom of this growth, though many did then. When the duel was prohibited by law, a gentleman in Tennessee asked, "What will become of honor?" That was over a hundred years ago, and, presumably, honor is neither dead nor without its strong champions in Tennessee. If democracy is not to slip back, it must forge ahead, forever working at the needs of ordinary people. As Plato foresaw, one of the most pressing problems in a democracy is that of securing and supporting the right kind of leadership. We can cite chapter and verse from our own history to illustrate the point that political leadership in a democracy is the pearl of great price for the demagogue. He is always on the lookout for opportunities to ingratiate himself with people as "their man." Actually, of course, there is only one effective way to keep him from reducing democracy to a form of totalitarianism, and that is to encourage the right kind of Christian laymen to seek and accept political responsibility. Obviously, we are not talking about someone who uses the social prestige of the church as a political springboard; we are talking about someone whose awareness of and loyalty to religious values can provide government with the moral stamina that a democracy must have or perish. But before those Christian laymen are willing to launch out on the uncertain seas of political fortune, they must have greater assurance of an aroused social conscience within and among churchmen generally than we have had to date. I cannot forget the answer given some of us who were asking a prominent Christian citizen to run for a high office: "I'm afraid I would be left in the lurch by church people when I would need them most!" Until and unless we can get our best Christian laymen to run for public offices and support them strongly, we shall be neglecting to build one of the strongest bridges between Christianity and democracy.

VI

There is yet a third way in which religion pours courage into the flagging democratic ideal. It helps cherish and cultivate many values that are as essential to democracy as to religion. Religion and democracy must of necessity hinder or help each other because they work on the same person at the same time. There is this difference between them, however: they work on different levels of that person's thought and life. Their vital relationship might be pictured this way: Their efforts parallel each other in principle on almost all issues. But they form a horizontal rather than vertical parallel in the life of any given person. Religion is the deeper line of the parallel, dealing with the universal implications of human life and thought. Democracy is the upper line of the parallel, dealing with the responsibility of the person to this particular segment of human life and society of which he is a part. Now, if religion is successful as it works at the lower level, democracy is strengthened. If democracy is successful as it works at the upper level, inevitably the significance of religion in human life is enormously enlarged. If democracy fails at the upper level, religion is weakened and hindered (but does not necessarily fail), though if religion fails at the lower level, democracy necessarily fails. That is why it is untrue to say that "democracy and religion stand or fall together." The meaning of this co-operation between the upper and lower levels of democracy and religion in personal life will be clarified if we see their efforts in operation in concrete cases.

1. Both democracy and religion find their surest guarantee for the future in their common answer to the query, What is man? Democracy's answer is found in the Declaration of Independence: "All men are created equal." That is *almost* a Christian answer. It would be entirely so if it read, "All men are created equal and *brothers one of another*." We are still waiting for the Christian answer to find its way as leaven through the law, institutions, and practices of this land that we love.

Ethical religion is duty-bound to challenge the right of some men to have more than they need while others have less than they need of the necessities of life. For democracy, this kind of injustice and inequity is a misreading of the constitutional effort to guarantee to all men the right to life, liberty, and the pursuit of happiness. For religion, it is a perversion of God's providence as we see it in the abundance of nature which man does not create, but appropriates for the nourishment of his own life. For one man to take more than he needs while another is unable to get as much as he needs is a misunderstanding of the worth and responsibility with which God has endowed every man. Christian ethics demand a rebuilding, not a redecoration, of life. And we have no right to claim exemption from that kind of radical reconstruction of life which must come about as we seek a more Christian social order. The task is clearly our Christian job; our work is cut out for us, and we must do everything in our power to see to it that this Christian gospel of the worth of the individual and the equality of all men in the sight of God becomes a molding force in our churches and throughout the entire social order.

2. Both religion and democracy agree that the individual must be kept conscious of the larger whole of which he is a part. Democracy visualizes this larger whole in terms of "general welfare" and "majority rule." Whenever we move into an election year we hear much of these conceptions. They underlie our constitutional practices. They remind us that we are parts of a larger whole and must conduct ourselves accordingly. Religion, working at the deeper level, likewise seeks to keep us conscious of a larger whole. But when it talks in terms of general welfare, it does not limit its concern to the citizens of this or any other nation. It is interested in the welfare of all men, in the brotherhood of man. Whereas democracy speaks of the will of the majority, religion speaks of the will of God. Religion talks in terms of the unity of all men everywhere in God, and seeks to awaken in the individual a keen consciousness of his relationship to and interdependence with this larger whole.

Neither democracy nor religion can tolerate any form of self-

sufficient individualism in which the individual defines himself
in opposition to the welfare of the larger whole. "Rugged individualism," as such, may have been possible in the days of the
pioneer era of this country's life; it may still be possible for a
Robinson Crusoe on his famous island, but its number has long
since been called in human history. Now we must bend our best
efforts toward finding the meaning of freedom within community. Religion's long experience—and tragic as well—in this area
enables it to be of great service to democracy. For religion has
been trying to persuade men for many centuries that they must
define their own welfare and freedom in terms of the welfare
and freedom of all men everywhere. So long as one man is in
chains anywhere on the face of the earth, we must confront the
fact of slavery; so long as one man is hungry somewhere, we must
seek to conquer the fact of hunger. A fair way to describe the
relationship is to say that what democracy seeks for the life of a
given people, religion seeks for mankind.

3. Then, too, both democracy and religion are interested in
broad-gauged, well-balanced lives for everyone. During the war
years, the ideal of strength was overdone so far as propaganda
was concerned. We know now that the youth of the country
must be trained in what is commonly called the foursquare life
if we are to have an enduring country. Democracy must do this
sort of thing since it stands or falls with the ability of the individual to measure up to the responsibilities of citizenship. Hence
the great interest in public education, in 4-H clubs, in parent-
teacher associations, and in many other specific efforts to awaken
in the citizens of a democracy a keen realization of their total
responsibility to it.

Religion is interested in the well-balanced personality, too.
To say this is not to ignore the fact that there have been times
when religion was the arch sinner against the well-balanced personality. For there was a time when it tried to divide man into
two parts, spirit and body, labeling spirit as all-important and
treating the body and its welfare as negligible. Then, too, there
have been times when we defined life so narrowly as to make

man a stranger, a sojourner here, telling him that his "home is far away beyond a golden strand." Slowly and surely we have come to see the error of such ways. They not only deny the unity of man's life, they question, if not blaspheme, God's judgment as Creator of life and earth. We, in religion, have learned the hard historical way that in nurturing the human personality we can do no better than be guided by the acute insight of the Gospel of Luke that "Jesus grew in wisdom and stature and in favor with God and man." As he grew, so ought all men to grow. Men must be the possessors of healthy bodies, minds, and spirits in order to bring to fulfillment the divine possibilities implanted within human life and history.

4. Democracy and religion alike seek to prepare a man to bear responsibility. Democracy does this in a thoroughgoing manner. It sets before every man the choice of a profession, of his life companion, of the kind of home he wants to have, of who his leaders in civic life shall be, of standards and values by which he will live, of the church in which he will be a member and seek to rear his children.

Religion seeks to train men to the point where they can bear the responsibility of making the over-all decisions for their life. It is important for us to realize that with all its exaltation of the supremacy of the will of God, it in no wise minimizes the importance of personal decision. Turn to the Old Testament strain, "Choose ye this day whom ye will serve"; or to the New Testament, "If any man will come after me, let him deny himself daily, take up his cross and follow me." These insights illustrate the manner in which every man must choose, and bear the responsibility of that choice. Martin Luther called this fact "the priesthood of all believers." Every man stands before God as a person and seeks to relate himself to the will of God; it is not necessary for him to have an intermediary in the form of a priest or a church through whom he makes his own peace with the will of God. Each man must bear full responsibility for his own relationship to that will. A man must answer to God, and to him more than anyone else, for the deepest decisions regarding the life that he lives. All the choices we make must finally square with the will of God for us and for all men who are affected by our choice—this is the stern admonition of religion.

5. Both democracy and religion emphasize the freedom of the individual and are gravely troubled about it. Mr. Walter Lippmann defines freedom, as we find it in democracy, in a very emphatic and somewhat negative way: "Freedom is the right to look any man in the eye and tell him to go to hell." I say this is a dramatic and somewhat negative version! Religion puts it positively but nonetheless dramatically, "Freedom is the right to look any man in the eye and hail him as brother." Neither religion nor democracy tolerates castes or inherited ranks. All honor accorded an individual must be in recognition of his own worth. This is the ideal of democracy and religion alike. We regard freedom as a virtue because it alone makes social and personal growth possible. This means that we shall treasure such fundamental freedoms as freedom of information, freedom of criticism, and freedom of creative energies and expressions. In no other way can we keep a social order or a church adjusted to the changing needs of a changing world.

Freedom takes another concrete form for both religion and democracy, one so hotly contested today that it deserves special mention. I refer to the freedom of a new idea or institution to win a following at the expense of accepted ideas and existing institutions. Since the latter framed the conventions and wrote the laws, the former has a hard time of it. One of the most pertinent examples of this tension is to be found in the fact that, today, it is accepted religious and legal doctrine south of the Rio Grande that evangelical churches shall not be permitted to win adherents from among those who are nominally related to the Roman Catholic Church. That kind of prohibition, of course, cuts across the fundamental meaning of freedom for both democracy and religion alike. If for some reason we desire to break away from a given political party or the established church, we must have the freedom both to do that and to win a following for what we are doing. This truth was never put more succinctly than when Lincoln observed that whenever the people of this country "grow weary of the existing government, they can exercise their constitutional right of amending it, or their revolutionary right to dismember or overthrow it."

I know of no way to maintain a strong emphasis upon freedom without opening doors that look in a direction that is dangerous in many respects. Even Lincoln's statement portrays this danger. But it is infinitely more dangerous to close those doors than it is to open them, especially in these days when freedom is on trial, when the right of free men to think out their problems and live their lives as seems best to them is being challenged the world around.

Another way to put the matter is to say that freedom is a virtue for both democracy and religion because conscience is a fact in human life and experience. When we speak of conscience, we are not talking about some abstract thing. We are talking about the ability of each individual to square up to the problems of his day, to take his own stand, and to feel that this is the proper thing to do. Conscience as such is the gift of God. It is the ability to glimpse in a flash of insight our total responsibility for the problem before us. Freedom of conscience, so conceived, is essential to the functioning of democracy and religion alike. When the Supreme Court rules, as it has with some frequency in these latter years, that the freedom of conscience must be subordinated to the will of the majority, thoughtful religionists gird on their spiritual armor and take the field at once. For the right of conscience is more than the possibility of social anarchy, it is the right to live as a human being.

VII

The Christian faith, then, makes three indispensable contributions to the survival of democracy. It strives to transform man until he becomes a fit citizen of a social order dedicated to the ideal of brotherhood. It strives to transform a social order until it both deserves and nurtures the life of such citizens. It stands at the side of the democratic ideal, cherishing and cultivating many of the same profound ideals and values. Canon F. R. Barry is speaking to both democracy and religion when he writes, "We are back on our ultimate ethical resources. What democracy needs for its survival is the leadership of spiritual conviction. Only so far as it is reestablished on its true moral and religious basis is there any hope that it can endure and move to the next stage in its development. All that we value most in our tradition is the gift of our ancestral Christianity; all we can hope to contribute to the future is inseparably bound up with it." [10]

The Christian religion stands far beyond the forms of democracy that we now enjoy, and says, "Come on up higher." It beckons to us, bogged down as we are in the racial antagonisms, the injustices, and other evils of our day, and says, "These must be conquered if you would live. They will not conquer themselves, but you have both the right and the power to master them before they master you." Mankind in general and this nation in particular, kept consciously under God, can achieve a much higher form of democracy than history has any record of to date. Washington saw this when, in his Farewell Address, he urged his fellow countrymen to pay constant and reverent attention to the worship of God. "Can it be," he asked, "that Providence has not connected the permanent felicity of a nation with its virtue?" Lincoln saw it when he said, "This nation, under God, shall have a new birth of freedom." Woodrow Wilson saw it in his *The Road Away from Revolution* when he said, "The sum of the whole matter is this, that our civilization cannot survive materially unless it is redeemed spiritually. It can be saved only by becoming permeated with the spirit of Christ and being made free and happy by the practices which spring out of that spirit. Only thus can discontent be driven out and all the shadows lifted from the road ahead." But each of these great leaders of democracy saw that we as individuals must sense our relationship and responsibility to God before we as a people can hope to fashion an enduring democracy. That is a step which no leader can take for us. But, under God, we can take it for ourselves if we lose not first our faith, then our courage.

Chapter VIII   ✺   A NEW CHURCH WORKS FOR A NEW WORLD

I

Most citizens of the twentieth century are so far away from the pastoral life in which the shepherd was a vital figure that it is easily misunderstood when applied to the Christian church. We do not, thereby, mean to imply that people are sheep. Most emphatically, we are not urging them to have sheepish reaction in these dangerous days. A quick glance at the actual life and work of the shepherd will explain why it is neither quietistic nor inappropriate to use it as a symbol of the work of the church today.

The job of the shepherd was a most necessary, exacting, and dangerous undertaking in ancient Israel. As outlined in Ezekiel, his work includes such strenuous undertakings as searching for lost sheep, driving off dangerous animals, and coping with thieves. In John, the same rigorous life is portrayed. The shepherd is to protect his fold from robbers, lead the sheep to proper pasture, and defend them against dangers. It is understandable that his job should rank high among difficult and honorable tasks. It called for understanding, shrewd, skillful, self-reliant, courageous men. We may be sure no Hebrew thought of looking down on the profession after David, the shepherd boy, became the great King of Israel.

It was inevitable, therefore, that the word "shepherd" should be used freely in a metaphorical sense. When Ezekiel wanted to denounce the priests who deserted their people, he called them "false shepherds." When he wanted to interpret the work of

God in a warm, moving symbol, he called Him "the Good Shepherd" who gathers His scattered, lost, and starving sheep to a place of safety. The one Psalm everybody knows begins, "The Lord is my shepherd; I shall not want. . . ." When Jesus describes his relationship to his disciples he says, "I am the good shepherd and know my sheep and am known of mine." And when he anticipates the glorious victory of his cause, he likens the triumphant Kingdom to one flock under one shepherd.

So when we liken the church to the shepherd we are not mapping out a serene and easy task. We are laying out a three-fold responsibility: (1) The church has the tremendously important responsibility of understanding and promoting the general welfare of all men; (2) the church has the inescapably dangerous responsibility of leading, protecting, combating evils of every sort that threaten the general welfare of men; (3) the church must lead its tired, torn, and quarreling peoples toward the fold of the spiritual unification of the world.

II

As the church desires to be a good shepherd, it will seek the general welfare of all men. The world is its field, its charge, its responsibility. Nothing human is alien to it. Every common task is "afire with God." It will regard all men—not just professing Christians—as belonging to the fold of God's people, "the sheep of His pasture." Some time ago a panel of speakers from the Federal Council of Churches was presenting the claims of the ecumenical church to an audience in Detroit. They were representing the church as the champion of "her people." At the conclusion of the presentation, during a question period, a non-Christian Chinese asked whether the church would be the champion of "her people" or of all people. There was only one possible answer: *all people*. We know that the divisions that separate men today are artificial, man-made, dangerous; that they are in direct violation of the will of Him in whose sight we are one. We cannot have or hope to have one flock until and unless we hold the welfare of all men in an even hand. Wherever men—any men—are in need, in distress of body, mind, or spirit, there is work for a good shepherd.

Nor is it difficult to translate the meaning of this from metaphorical into highly practical terms. Where men are in need of education, the church must either build the schools or keep everlastingly after the civil authorities until they build them. Wherever men are in need of better housing, the church cannot and must not think of rest until she has helped bring into existence the answer to their need. In this same spirit, we can run the appallingly long gamut of remediable social needs: health protection, old-age pensions, unemployment insurance, playgrounds for children, equality before the law and at the polls, etc. Where men are threatened by tyranny, the church must stand for freedom; by lawlessness, for order; by immorality, for purity. Where men are denied justice, are being broken in body, mind, or spirit by inequities, the church must stand by and for them, must suffer with them, until justice and equity are done.

Against some such realistic background as this the statement can be made that, so far from being outmoded, the Christian faith is probably better prepared than any other part of our civilization for this new age of internationalism into which we have been thrust by the relentless forces of history. The clear intent of its message and the equally clear unfolding of its mission in history stamp it as internationally minded, in the highest and best sense of that term.

The church has taken the world as its parish both because of the great commission from Jesus to "go to the uttermost parts of the earth" and because of the inexorable thrust toward universality implicit in the essentials of the Christian faith. Consider these affirmations: (1) we believe in God as Creator, Sustainer, Redeemer of the world; (2) we believe in Jesus Christ as the clearest revelation of the will of God for the life of mankind; (3) we believe in man as the child of God, created, sustained, and redeemed in His holy love; (4) we believe in the church as the "family of God." Where in these is there room for the sectarian divisions that rend Christendom asunder, for dividing mankind into "inferior and superior" races, into "privileged and dispossessed" peoples?

No one knows better than a student of church history how grievously the church has failed to live up to the highest insights of this great commission. The fruits of failure are in evidence on every hand today. Let the church set a good example and make proper confession of sin on certain major points.

The first confession is this: religion has proved to be one of the most divisive forces in human history. Has any enterprise on the face of the earth taught brotherhood and love more constantly and practiced intolerance and bigotry more widely than religious institutions?

A second confession is equally grim: religion is guilty of parochialism, of paying too much attention to narrowly restricted fields of religious interest. When we talk about our church, we mean our local church, never our denomination, let alone world Christianity. We do our thinking in terms of a particular church and its particular problems. Fortunately, here and there among us are people who keep their eyes fixed on the far horizons of world responsibility and, let us hope, they tend to leaven the lump.

There is a third confession: religion has been guilty of reinforcing nationalism the world over. Almost inevitably we discover ourselves at the task of defending the *status quo* in which the roots of our institution have extended and upon which we seem to depend for life. When the Hebrews were nomads roaming from oasis to oasis, their god was their chieftain. They looked to Moses for leadership in the wilderness because they believed he had special access to Yahweh, the God who had promised to lead them safely by day and by night to the Promised Land. It seems never to have occurred to them to doubt that the will of God was identified with the welfare of their tribe. Although later Jewish thinkers did trim back some of the crudities of this early notion, its vital center lived on in the idea that the Jews were the "Chosen People" of God, His peculiar treasure among the nations of the earth. That this belief was a source of strength in adversity is obvious to all students of Jewish history. But, unfortunately, it was more than an incentive to courage: it was an invitation to pride. All too many became less and less concerned about their special mission as a people and more and more intoxicated with the pride and sense of spiritual superiority which came almost naturally with the conviction that they were the "darlings of deity." Although their prophets, now as then, rebuked this smugness, it has never been absent from Jewish life. But Christians are in no position to judge them too severely in this matter. We have inherited and Christianized, so far as possible, this doctrine of a chosen people. And, what is worse, we have sought both to nationalize and to Christianize it at one and the same time. The evidence of this is sickeningly recent; every embattled nation in the recent war identified the cause of the Christian faith with its victory.

We begin, then, our consideration of the relationship of religion to internationalism with this simple confession of obvious sin. However, the record is not one of unrelieved sinfulness. There are many achievements in it and they are of great importance.

One of the longest steps toward internationalism or universalism was taken by the prophets of ancient Israel in their belief that one God, a God of justice and righteousness for all men, controls the destinies of all people. That vision of God, insisted upon seven hundred years before Christ, has since been one of the touchstones of Jewish-Christian ethics. It visualizes a universal God, whose will is seen in nature, history, and human destiny. He is not the peculiar possession of any one people. He is the Creator and Preserver of all peoples everywhere who turn to Him.

The second noteworthy achievement of religion is the insistence that the ideal of the brotherhood of man must be treated not as a fancy but as a fact. It is reality-thinking, not fantasy-thinking, to adopt Freud's terminology. Fortunately, the scientists are helping with this point now. No biologist denies the basic physiological likeness of all men. No physiologist seeks to deny that men have the same general biological equipment, the same needs, the same desires. We ask of life the same general reward, regardless of who or where we are. There is a basic oneness among all men. Those of us who believe in the brotherhood of man raise this question: are we going to be able to bring to birth in the thought and the plans of men the ethical and logical conclusion to this basic oneness we find in mind, body, and social relationships? Are we going to be able to bring into realization through institutions and creative social planning this oneness, the foundation of which is so firmly laid in body, mind, and society? The ideal of the brotherhood of man is no beautiful daydream projected on the rosy clouds of an intangible future. It confronts us and the world in which we live as the one great and good fact upon which we can proceed as we move into an otherwise ominous future. Like the pearl of great price, it is at hand; like the Kingdom of God, it is growing all around us, even within us! As one writer in the Old Testament has put it, "Have we not all one Father? Hath not one God created us? Why do we deal treacherously every man against his brother?" There is the problem, and grapple with it we must if we would survive the age in which we live. "Why do we deal treacherously every man against his brother?" The answer we give to that question will determine in large measure the course taken by human history in the immediate future, and if we get the wrong answer, there will be no human history in the distant future!

A third contribution of religious faith to internationalism is the world mission of the Christian religion, which as much as anything else has served to awaken us to the reality of the unity of the whole world. One glance at any map showing the extent of the missionary programs of the Christian churches will reveal, not a parochial concern, but a world-wide undertaking. I well remember a map of church missions that hung on the wall of the church school which I attended as a boy. It was dotted with a number of pins, each one of which indicated a mission station. We were told that in these stations various people were at work preaching the gospel: some were preachers, some teachers, some doctors, some instructors in farming. I think I have never seen a more fascinating map because, better than anything else, it was the symbol of something going on all over the world, something in which I could share if I chose to do so.

In simple truth, despite its deplorable concordats with nationalism, the Christian church, as a whole, has a most impressive record for internationalism. Consider it in geographical terms and you will get some notion of its sweep in human history. Palestine, Greece, Rome, North Africa; Europe, North America, South America, Asia; every continent and most of the islands of the seven seas—this is the home, the world parish, of the Christian church. Consider it in human terms: Every shade of color, every language and almost every dialect have known the name of Christ and heard the invitation to share in the creation of his Kingdom on earth. So far from being a paper internationalism, you can feel it as a living reality in the corporate life of the church itself. At any general conference of the Methodist Church, for example, there will be representatives from every corner of the globe and from every race known to man. They will meet together to think, plan, and act as a world Christian church. At the first meeting of the World Council of Churches in 1948 every portion of the family of God will be represented. In fact, one of the most impressive things about the World Council of Churches which is taking form these days is that it will include almost one-half of all the professing Christians of the world. Many decades will elapse before it becomes the powerful world voice it is destined to be, but a good start has been made and, with the continued support of the great church bodies of this and other countries, it cannot fail. It is already grappling with problems of meeting human need on a world-wide scale, the spiritual reconstruction of Europe, training new Christian leadership for the evangelization of Europe, helping in many ways to make the church a more potent instrument for good in public affairs. It points to the day when the creedal and racial divisions in Christian churches will belong to the past, when there will be no "national" churches, even in name, but all will be truly international in character and program.

This intrinsic and unfolding internationalism of the Christian church better fits it for the present age than for the two immediately preceding ones. The sixteenth, seventeenth, and early eighteenth centuries constitute the age of nationalism. During this period the various regional, cultural, and, in some cases, racial and religious divisions of Europe and the West were organizing themselves as political entities called national states. It was a long, bitter, bloody process and the net historical result was the creation of a number of centers of power that were forever suspicious of one another and always trying to become greater and more powerful, usually at the expense of other nations but also by extending their sway over less powerful peoples in other portions of the world. They regarded the so-called heathen areas of the world as a farmer regards his milk cows.

The age of nationalism with its inevitable tendencies toward expansion led to the age of imperialism in the latter part of the eighteenth century and all of the nineteenth. The great powers of Europe established their domination over the most profitable parts of the world. Because there were more points of rivalry and acute tension, the wars between the great powers began to increase in numbers and intensity, and a great shadow began to gather over Western civilization—the shadow of world-wide catastrophe. Neither nationalism nor imperialism were unmixed blessings to mankind! To be sure, they did mingle blessings with their curses, but it became clear that in the long run they were going to envelop humanity in a bloody fate.

There is reason to believe that the conscience of religion was deeply disturbed by the limited, parochial outlook of these ages and sought to counterbalance their invitation to doom by launching the mightiest missionary enterprise known to history. Dr. Kenneth Scott Latourette calls the nineteenth century "the Great Century" for the church because it saw the parochialism of the Western world challenged to final combat by the universalism of the Christian faith. That struggle is not yet over. We do not know who will win in the end, but things have not been going too well for the efforts of the church in view of what has been happening in the twentieth century. Lenin rightly called modern history "one bloody lump." But it ought to give us confidence for our task to realize that the church rose to the challenge of the previous ages and by so doing has fitted itself for the one-world age which is here and here to stay.

This new age has one great need that the Christian faith can meet as no other religion can. That is the need for new goals for nations and peoples to strive for. Peoples, like individuals, are always in motion, always going somewhere at a given time in their history. They may reverse and contradict themselves, but they never stand still. The ends that were sought in the previous ages are admittedly inadequate since they were predicated upon the false assumption of the superiority of race, or nation, or class. The new ends to be sought must be all-embracing and utterly fundamental in character. Professor Sorokin says that the crisis of our age is to be found in the fact that we have been unwilling or afraid to move toward new goals. He continues, and without hesitation, to single out the universalism of the Christian faith as containing the true goals of a genuinely new age. Another prominent man—whose experience lies everywhere but in a classroom—reaches the same conclusion. General MacArthur, during the surrender ceremonies in Tokyo Bay, spoke these now-familiar words: "We have had our last chance. If we do not now devise some greater and more equitable system, Armageddon will be at our door. The problem basically is theological and involves a spiritual recrudescence and improvement of human character. It must be of the spirit if we are to save the flesh."

The church, then, is the Good Shepherd when it tries to take care of all its sheep, all God's people. For it must never forget that it is the humble servant of God. This fact was driven home with the greatest possible eloquence by the stumbling words of a native chieftain on an island in the South Seas by the name of Jason. He and his tribe—all Christians—had built a chapel commemorating the sixteen hundred American men who fell in battle there. As Jason presented the chapel to the American chaplain he said, "We want tell you all people that we fella belong Solomon build this church because we want thank you. Now we give this church you. But this church no belong you and me. This church belong God!"

III

Who can doubt that as the church seeks to be a Good Shepherd it has a vital and dangerous responsibility? For, as champion of the welfare of all men, it has arrayed against it all the evil forces known to man and society. Few people question the worth and the need of the philanthropic and educational institution of the church now, though they were fought tooth and nail when they were inaugurated. Our hospitals and homes, our orphanages and schools are inseparable parts of the church life now. But when the church throws its resources against the many enemies that either openly or secretly threaten the spiritual welfare of its people, it encounters all sorts of opposition and enmity. Like its Master, the church has found and will find itself despised and rejected by some men because of its very determination to be the spokesman for all needy peoples.

We know who the open enemies of the human spirit are. We have been locked in mortal combat with them for a long time now—and the end is not yet.

Tyranny—that foe of the free mind, the inquiring spirit, the clear conscience, the individual commitment—we have met incarnate in Neros and Hitlers since the days of Peter and Paul. There can be no compromise with it whether it comes to us with clenched fists and threats or with outstretched hands and comfortable invitations to let it do our thinking. God-given abilities like reason and conscience cannot and must not be surrendered to the management of anyone else no matter how wise or good he may seem to be.

Slavery is another open foe. When the ideal of brotherhood began to take form in Christian thought and life, the end of slavery was assured. Much has been accomplished by and through the church toward this end. But the work is far from finished. We are learning now that no man is really free until he can face the future with reasonable confidence in the welfare of himself and those dependent upon him. Although legal enslavement is a thing of the past everywhere, many of its most damaging aspects live on in institutions and conventions that are determined to preserve the fruits of discrimination without losing the appearance of equity. As Bishop Alexander Shaw of the Central Jurisdiction of the Methodist Church told the Preachers' Meeting of Baltimore, "You have done the really big thing for my people when you set us free. Now all we want are some little things like a place to build our homes, and jobs, and schools, and a chance to live like other people." Thank God, he eased the burden that crushed his hearers by smiling as he spoke those words! Little things! A place to build their homes! (We white people of Baltimore have hounded a Negro housing project from one suburb to another, wanting the Negroes to have good homes all right, but not in any known place!) A job! A good school! No man can live without these today. They are of the essence of freedom.

Poverty is another open foe of the human spirit. It will gnaw away at a man's self-respect and self-confidence as the waves eat away rocks on a shore. It makes no difference whether it hits a family in the South, the North, the East, or the West. It is the same whether the man is a minister, or dentist, or laboring man. During the depression of the early thirties, a play was presented on the New York stage which portrayed a dentist starving because all about him people who needed his services had no money with which to get them. One after another his clients—his livelihood—went into the soup lines of that city. The dentist's pride would not let him do that. Finally, in desperation, he turned his eyes to the heavens and prayed, in effect, "Oh God, haven't you any use for me at all?" Poverty does that to men.

And it does even worse things to children! The Y.M.C.A. of Baltimore started a day camp for underprivileged boys a few years ago. I recall taking some boys out to it one lovely morning in June. They were from the slums of the city and were fascinated at the prospect. They said little as the green and rolling countryside of our beautiful state sped by. When we got to the camp, we heard the shouts of other boys at play all over the place. Some of the boys from my car disappeared like a flash, but one hung back, just looking. Finally I said to him, "It's all yours for the day. Have a good time." He asked with a voice of unbelief, "Can I run anywhere, Mister?" Then, for the first time, I think I really saw and heard the slums of Baltimore! I got the feel of his daily life as never before: crowded home, streets for playgrounds, little gangs gathering here and there to be dispersed by the police. What a contrast it was to the broad vista of a countryside where he could do what he pleased!

When the depression was paralyzing Chicago in the 1930's, I was asked to talk to a group of unemployed men who were gathered together once a week through the efforts of Arthur Holt and some of his colleagues. I tried to point to some rays of hope in our dark world, but when the speech was over one man said in a voice of quiet despair, "You fellows mean all right, but you hold our hands while the bosses pick our pockets."

The Christian church cannot and will not make peace with poverty. If the struggle against it must go on for ten thousand years, it will go on until victory is won, until the good earth becomes a place of plenty for all of the children of God. To even think of stopping short of this is an outright betrayal of the Christian gospel.

War is the fourth member of this quartet of open enemies of the human spirit. Involving as it does the conscription of body, mind, and spirit for the purposes of destruction, it is evil. If it be not evil, then nothing is or can be evil. All our justifications of it, whether facile or just frenzied, get their answer in the simple, unanswerable fact that all the goods of life are impoverished by it and all the evils of life are multiplied by it. Though a church— even a great church—changes its verbal statements about war from condemnation to quasi approval, it cannot change this fundamental fact about the nature of war itself. How long is it going to be before Christian churches take seriously the condemnation of war which comes from the men who know it best? General Eisenhower speaking at Ottawa, Canada, in January, 1946, said, "War is always negative. The best we can do is get rid of it. . . . I hate war as only a soldier who has lived in it

can, as one who has seen its brutality, its futility, its stupidity."
When this great soldier was receiving an honorary degree at the
Boston University in February, 1946, he said, "I have been classed
as a rather risky chance-taking person, and I venture to make a
suggestion. Why doesn't Dr. Marsh [President of Boston Uni-
versity], and the president of every great university in the world,
teach his people to put people in my profession permanently out
of a job?"

Until today, only Christian pacifists dared call for the immediate and absolute abolition of war as an instrument of national
policy. Now, a host of voices demand it. General MacArthur
stirs the conscience of the world with his impassioned plea for the
abolition of war. President Robert Hutchins of the University of
Chicago has stated our task with terrifying simplicity, "There is
no defense against the atomic bomb . . . we shall have to beat
war . . . we cannot beat the atomic bomb, therefore we must
beat war." [1] When Mr. Bernard Baruch presented the American
plan to internationalize atomic power to the Atomic Energy
Commission of the United Nations on June 14, 1946, he began
with these ominous words, "Before a country is ready to re-
linquish any winning weapon, it must have more than words to
reassure it. It must have a guarantee of safety, not only against
offenders in the atomic area, but against the illegal users of other
weapons. . . . In the elimination of war lies our solution. . . .
Let this be anchored in our minds: peace is never long preserved
by weight of metal or by an armament race. Peace can be made
tranquil and secure only by understanding and agreement forti-
fied by sanctions. We must embrace international cooperation or
international disintegration." [2]

Testimonies like these make us realize that the Paris Peace Pact
to outlaw war may have been a faulty instrument but it was looking in the right direction. What it tried to do must finally be done
or we perish at our own hand. Consequently, we are but stating
a truism when we say that the Christian church cannot rest until
war is no more. Our testimony against it must be firm, unequivo-
cal, and strong.

Unfortunately, not all of the enemies of the flock of the Good Shepherd are as easily spotted as tyranny, slavery, poverty, and war. There are others and they deserve to be called by name: *materialism*, or the view that life is essentially a matter of food and drink; *special privilege*, or the philosophy that one is entitled to all that he can get and keep by whatever means; *fatalism*, the attitude of "Why be so concerned about life? What is to be, is to be!" Undoubtedly many others could be added to this list, but these suggest the nature of the enemies that sift their way silently and unseen into the lives and hearts of people and tear the flock asunder before they are controlled.

Take materialism as an example of how such enemies try to masquerade as friends of the flock, even as aids to the Good Shepherd. The Good Shepherd is interested in the physical welfare of his flock, their food and drink. He will labor endlessly to make these possible for them because life without the basic necessities is unthinkable. Materialism takes advantage of the fact that people must spend much time providing for the physical side of life, and it begins to insinuate that the Kingdom of God is a matter of eating and drinking properly and regularly. To a hungry or thirsty man this sounds plausible enough. But the church must remind him that "Man does not live by bread alone, but by every word that proceedeth out of the mouth of God." In the devastated areas of the world, food, clothing, shelter, and medicines are desperately needed, and should be given. Thus far the materialist and the man of faith stand side by side. But other things are needed just as desperately: confidence, dignity, fellowship, honor, brotherhood. Whatever we take by way of material goods to the needy peoples of Europe or Asia (and we ought to take all we can) must be taken in the hand of fellowship. When the four churchmen went from America to Japan at the conclusion of the war, they asked a number of Japanese Christians what was most needed in that country and one of the answers was, "Your prayers!" Let others go, if they must, as victors among vanquished, but let churchmen either go as brothers among brethren —or stay at home!

Special privilege speaks up on almost every occasion from within the fold asking for added consideration. Sometimes it is the self-styled "advanced races" of the world saying with serious face and long-suffering demeanor that they have an "obligation" to continue to control dependent peoples until they are capable of acting independently. The Good Shepherd will rip open the sophistry of that claim and expose the corruption in motive and deed which underlies it. The churches of Great Britain have done just that as regards the Tory claim that England must continue to rule India "for India's own good." They have been among the stanchest supporters of the present Labor government's effort to shift control from Whitehall to Delhi. And the American churches must do no less than our British brethren when our own industrial imperialists begin to tell us about the advantages that the Orient will reap if and when they begin to trade with us. They are but trying to add some more cows to their own herd.

Imperialism is a species of tyranny and as such stands condemned by the Christian conscience and must be opposed by the Christian church in all parts of the world. Dr. Paul Hutchinson points out that we must make our choice between imperialism and missions.[3] If the missionary enterprise is to be continued, the Christian churches in America must persist in the stand taken at Cleveland in 1945:

Long and intimate relationships with the dependent peoples of Africa, Southeast Asia, and other parts of the world, place on the Christian Churches a responsibility to champion their right to freedom and to develop their capacity for self-government.

We therefore call upon our government and others: (1) to proclaim self-government as the goal for all dependent peoples; (2) where dependent peoples are ready for self-government, to give it now; (3) otherwise, to initiate progressive steps suitable for each area for achieving that goal; and (4) in the interim to provide that all such areas shall be administered under the supervision of world organization.

We cannot in good conscience be a party to the dismantling of Japanese colonial possessions without at the same time insisting that the imperialism of the white man shall be brought to the speediest possible end. We cannot have a sound or stable world community so long as there is enforced submission of one people to the will of another whether in Korea, in India, in the Congo, in Porto Rico or anywhere else.[4]

Just now special privilege is being sought by the state in every area of life. The state says that it can determine what should and should not be taught in public schools. The proposal is frequently heard these days that we "ought to be more careful" about what is taught in our public institutions. It is easy to share that concern without sharing the prejudices which prompt it upon all too many occasions. It is the business of the church to be our conscience in this matter and to remind us that Truth should be the determining factor of what is taught, not what a society may want taught at any given time. Although we recognize the very great difficulty of determining precisely what the truth is in such disputed areas as history and economics, the plain fact remains that a social order must either pretend it has the truth or give the schools the right to investigate all possible avenues which might lead toward a greater truth than any now in existence. It will be a sorry day for public education if and when the public schools become simply centers of indoctrination, as many prominent people are beginning to say they should be. What is not clearly perceived is that where indoctrination flourishes, investigation languishes. Schools ought to be centers of investigation primarily and centers of indoctrination secondarily, if at all. Yet to say this is to run counter to the growing demand on the part of the state that it be permitted to determine what shall be taught in the public schools.

Then, too, the modern state reasons that because it grants the church freedom of worship, the church should stand squarely behind it no matter what it does. When I hear this idea advanced either directly or indirectly, whether in time of peace or in time of war, I am reminded of a conference a number of us had with an attaché of the German Embassy in Washington in 1939. We were seeking firsthand information about the relationship between the German churches and the Third Reich. The man to whom we were speaking said, "The Churches are getting along

all right. One or two of their leaders are in trouble but that is because they misunderstand the proper relationship between the
Church and State in Germany." When we inquired what that
was, he said, "So long as the Church is supported by the State,
the State has a right to expect the support of the Church." During the recent war, the churches' great reluctance to support the
war was an object of considerable criticism. I had it pointed out
to me several times that we in churches ought to be grateful to
the government for permitting freedom of worship here. How
widespread this idea is in our secular and pagan society I do not
know. But apparently, it is widespread enough for the church to
point out that it won the right to freedom of worship long before
the Constitution was ever thought of, and won it by right of im-
migration and settlement in America in colonial days. Naturally,
we want to be properly grateful for its inclusion in the basic law
of the land, but, know it for a fact, it would never have appeared
there had it not first demonstrated its worth in life.

When the church fights these open and secret enemies of the
general welfare, it will find arrayed against it, more often than
not, many of the most powerful resources of society: the great
daily papers of the cities, the radio, and the constant pressure of
criticism of many influential people. But we must never forget
that we are to care for the welfare of all people, not just our
people or our nation. That is the task of the Good Shepherd.
Here is what the Cleveland Conference of the Commission on
World Order says about this matter:

The Christian Church can recognize no political nor racial limits to
its responsibility for human welfare; there is no area from which its
activity can be excluded on the ground that it is a domestic concern.
By its primary authority, Jesus Christ, by its oldest directive, and by
its uninterrupted and world-inclusive action, the Church has accepted
and seeks to exercise its fullest moral responsibilities for man's welfare
without distinction of nation or race.[5]

This, again, is the voice of the Good Shepherd who knows his
sheep and is known to them.

IV

You have a right to ask how the church can hope to lead the tired, worn, and quarreling peoples of the world toward one spiritual goal when it is so badly rent itself by dissension. That question ought to be uppermost in the minds of every Christian leader because it assuredly is uppermost in the minds of thoughtful people inside as well as outside the church. Canon Charles Raven discovered this through a painful experience which he himself relates. He had been having a cordial conversation with a businessman in Liverpool who was assisting in the building of the cathedral there. Their conversation had strayed from the work of the cathedral to the then-threatening general strike and the groping efforts of the League of Nations at Geneva to bring some sort of stability into the world situation. As they rose to go, the businessman said, "One moment, padre. There's one thing I must say. *You're a damned fraud.* You come here talking about the need for friendship at Geneva and for masters and men to collaborate in industry. When I find Anglicans and Romans and Presbyterians and Methodists and Congregationalists and Baptists and Unitarians and Quakers and the Salvation Army and the rest of you Christians meeting and collaborating here in Liverpool, I'll feel that you have some right to expect others to do so. Till then you're a hypocrite—and you know it." [6] Of course this is an exaggeration, but, unfortunately, it exaggerates in the direction of truth—and that truth implicates us all. What the plain-spoken layman did not see was that, in so far as he was a faithful churchman, he, too, was a fraud! It is not difficult to find laymen and ministers alike who deplore "disunion." But it is hard to find many who will accept its conquest as one of the major tasks of the contemporary church. Dr. Theodore Wedel in his fine book, *The Coming Great Church,*[7] demands that we face this fact of disunion squarely as a major sin. "Familiarity has robbed the sin of disunion of its shame," he warns. It is a striking thing that the missionary churches, the so-called younger churches, are the ones who are agitating most strongly for an immediate effort to heal the ancient schisms that separate the various branches of Christianity. They do not see the importance of perpetuating the sixteenth-century controversy, Dr. Wedel thinks. "And why should they?" he asks. They have just accepted Christ, and they are nearer to the New Testament church than to the post-Reformation church. To them, faith in Christ, not in the forms of some branch of the church, is the most important thing. Many years ago Dr. E. Stanley Jones startled us by saying that India wants our Christ but not our Christianity. This is a damning indictment of our churchmanship. Certainly if there is something about the church that cannot be presented along with the Christ, we must of necessity recognize it as secondary and treat it accordingly. That, as I understand it, is precisely what the ecumenical movement is trying to do for the contemporary church.

One way of stating the magnitude of the task of the ecumenical movement is to say that it is an attempt to bridge the chasms that have been slowly widening among Christian sects over four centuries. The quarrelsome sins of our quarrelsome religious forefathers were at least three hundred years old before the church began seriously to move toward a new unity. The ecumenical movement is now about fifty years old. It has been gaining great momentum since 1937.[8] It stands before us today with concrete and rapidly expanding achievements to its credit. Its purpose is to make of all Christian sects integral members of the family of God. Its achievements to date are impressive enough to cause great hope for increasing communion where once there was only conflict among the various branches of Christendom. There is real encouragement in the fact that the great statesmen of the contemporary church have given and are giving liberally of their time to the furtherance of this work. But effort at the top of the ecclesiastical hierarchy is not enough by itself. The will and the move toward communion across the chasms between churches must grow in strength in local churches or the whole ecumenical movement will die a-borning. When, and only when, the men and women, lay and ministerial, in the Christian churches of the world are willing to work for interchurch communion with as much vigor as they now work for their own denomination will the movement get the grass-roots' power and reality it hopes to have and must have if it is to succeed. The vast and effective promotional apparatus of the great churches should devote at least as much time to this work as to their own sectarian concerns. Important as it is to maintain the Methodist or Baptist or Presbyterian churches in strength in this country, it is not more important (I should say, it is far less important) than that the ecumenical movement should grow in great strength—and rapidly. The great churches must take seriously their own responsibility in the achievement of "the Great Church." And if they must say, like John the Baptist, it ". . . must increase, I must decrease," so be it!

Common sense dictates that we make every effort to strengthen the churches now in existence. But let them be strengthened at those points and on those issues where they sustain and support each other. Dr. Wedel is hopeful that we are actually moving in this direction now: "A world-wide community is discovering its existence, and giving to that existence outward and visible signs. A people of God is forming once more, seeing itself as one in time with that people of God to which . . . God once made promise for all times." [9]

The ecumenical movement will really get strength in the lives of ordinary people when individual ministers, local church boards, and church school teachers take some such stand as this: "I am a member of the Christian Church which is seeking to express itself here and now through the Methodist [read any other] Church in which I work and serve. I shall do nothing in behalf of the Methodist Church which will weaken the Great Church but will do everything that will serve to make the Methodist Church a more fitting embodiment of the Christian Church!" This makes each Christian guardian of a sacred trust—the One Church. But it is not a trust to be guarded as a thing apart from ordinary living; it is a seed to be planted in the soil of that living, to be tended with all diligence and wisdom until "the family of God" becomes an apt symbol of mankind.

But the task to which this resolution leads is staggering. Deep as are the fissures between and among Protestant Christian groups, they are nothing as ominous as those between Protestantism and Roman Catholicism; while these in turn are much more "bridge-able" than those between Christian and non-Christian faiths. Not a few of us become fainthearted at the total prospect. But progress is being made in each case. The Great Church is coming like the dawn silently supplanting the night, but it is coming.

I do not see how any fair-minded person can study the rapid growth of the ecumenical movement in contemporary Christian thought and life and doubt that "the Great Church" is coming. Such books as *The Christian Basis of World Order*,[10] *A Christian Global Strategy*,[11] and *Christian World Mission* [12] testify to the realism with which the Christian conscience is facing the problems of our age. There is an almost miraculous determination to find a basis for unity and spiritual community among the scattered branches of the Christian church. While rightly suspicious of zealous attempts to force a premature and superficial unity, we may entertain an even greater suspicion of any effort to set the limit beyond which the ecumenical movement may not go.[13] Dr. E. Stanley Jones is calling for a federal union of churches that will bring the various sects into a vital co-operative relationship with one another.[14] He proposes that it be called the Church of Christ in America and operate in a truly catholic spirit, providing ample freedom for denominational and doctrinal differences yet creating the vehicle for implementing the many powerful facts upon which there is complete agreement among the churches. Dr. Walter van Kirk argues that the time is ripe for us to "throw precedent and pride of race to the wind and create a World Board of Christian Strategy that will truly represent all racial and national groups . . ." [15] This board would be an instrument through which the World Council of Churches actually thinks, plans, and acts as a World Council.

Thinking like this is going on all over Christendom now—and is one of the most hopeful signs that the church will rise to its high calling as Shepherd of all His sheep. To be sure, the power of inertia, of settling back into the rut from which we were rudely and tragically jarred a few years ago, must not be under-estimated. There are those who want to get back to "normalcy" in churches as well as in other areas of life! But most of us know that the ways back are closed, closed forever and closed by the hand of God in human history. Henceforth we live—if we are to live at all—toward the future or, more accurately, facing the fu-ture as it unfolds in and through the present. This does not mean that hard-won and time-tested tradition and illuminating insights are to be scrapped. No intelligent person thinks for a moment that this can safely be done. But it does and must mean that, in Ranke's words, we realize that we are living "directly to God." It means that there will be a winnowing of the wheat of tradition, even precious theological and ecclesiastical tradition. It means that re-ligious faith will seek to impregnate the world with its vision and courage rather than cultivate this vision in isolation from the problems that men face.

Josiah Royce has a masterly condensation of the philosophy of Hegel which contains this description of Hegel's Absolute: "[He is] no God that hides himself behind clouds and darkness, nor yet a Supreme Being who keeps himself carefully clean and untroubled in the recesses of an inaccessible divinity. No, Hegel's Absolute is a man of war. The dust and the blood of ages of humanity's life are upon him; he comes before us pierced and wounded, but triumphant—the God who has conquered contra-dictions and who is simply the total spiritual consciousness that expresses, embraces, unifies, and enjoys the whole wealth of our human loyalty, endurance, and passion." [16]

This, better than anything outside the Bible, suggests the sheer realism of the actual work of the Christian church. So far from finding its way around problems, it must find its way to their heart. Instead of skirting controversial issues, it must determine as best, as speedily, and as humbly as it can where the will of

God leads and then join the struggle. James Hayden Tufts once said, "There is no room for spectators in the arena of life." In its great days the church has known this to be true and has acted accordingly. With God's help this can be another in that glorious succession of "great days." Know it for a fact that if we should fail to do our part in this high endeavor, it will be the last day of our efforts to create a Christian civilization.

Chapter IX　　　❧　　　"WHILE TIME
REMAINS"

I

There has never been any doubt as to what constitutes the great commission of the Christian faith: It is to take
the gospel to the ends of the earth. From that incredible day
nearly two thousand years ago when Jesus Christ first gave it to
a handful of anxious, fearful disciples until today when those
who name his name are numbered by the hundreds of millions,
the historical mission of the Christian fellowship has been one
and the same. True enough, as Dr. Kenneth S. Latourette points
out,[1] this mission has advanced much more rapidly in some generations than others. Indeed, in some it seems actually to have lost
ground. But the awareness of it was never wholly lacking in even
the darkest days of Christian history. The primary task of the
Christian church has been and remains the evangelization of the
world, the final achievement in history of that time "when every
knee shall bow and every tongue confess" the name of our Lord
and Saviour. Underlying the dismaying disunity of the various
Christian groups today is complete accord on this ultimate aim
and objective of the Christian faith in history. It is the common
center toward which they move as they learn to think, pray, and
work together.

There is a peculiar urgency in the great commission just now.
Diagnosticians of contemporary culture tell us that their patient
is sick—very sick. So sick, in fact, that there is only a slight chance
for recovery—and some are dubious of even that!

H. G. Wells, for example, has gone on record as believing that

176

there is no way out for our civilization, that the destructive forces now on the loose are too numerous and too powerful for us to hope to control them. Dr. Pitiran Sorokin says that "We are living in the bloodiest crisis of the bloodiest century in human history." Dr. Paul Hutchinson writes of "the sense of encroaching chaos which fills every thoughtful mind with apprehension if not despair. . . ." General MacArthur warns us that "Armageddon will be at our door." The editors of *Time* say we are "on final ground." Mr. Raymond Fosdick says, "We have had our last chance." In fact, circumstances are so parlous that we find a vice-presidential address given to the American Academy for the Advancement of Science closing with an honest and earnest invocation of Deity: "May God give those in authority the wisdom to erect a just international structure that the world may shortly attain to a lasting peace." [2] The eminent scientists who wrote *It's One World or No World* leave no doubt in our mind that that title is a literal description of the choice before us now.

Dr. Paul Hutchinson, in his *The New Leviathan* [3] tells of a badly scared newspaper editor in Illinois who proposes to do something drastic to ward off the impending doom. Believing that our heads have developed too far beyond our hearts, he favors having the government reduce all public school teachers' salaries to $500 a year and public school classes to one hour a week, while it pays all ministers $20,000 a year and all Sunday school superintendents $10,000 and forces all citizens to attend church schools five days a week! [4] We need not share this editor's notion of a proper remedy in order to agree with him that something drastic must be done and done now. It is painfully apparent that we have no such endless amount of time for the task of rebuilding society on new spiritual foundations as we once thought we had. That idea died on August 6—it was the first casualty at Hiroshima. We know beyond all doubt that "It's one world or no world"; it's now or never.

Though the urgency is greater, the task we face is no easier. It is easy enough to sing, "We've a story to tell to the nations," but it has proved appallingly difficult to get nations into a receptive frame of mind. Nothing that has happened since August 6, 1945, indicates that the major powers are playing other than power politics in their efforts to check each other or in seeming to play the friend of small nations. Even President Truman, although warning us in one breath that there must be no more war, says, in the next, that with the war over we can now indulge in "politics as usual"! The struggle for power in industry, in labor, and between management and labor goes on with few if any indications of the imminence of complete chaos for our entire civilization. Churchmen, educators, and many editors seem to be more oppressed by the shortness of time, but as yet they have not been able to get the average listener or reader stirred to creative action about it.

In fact, what is going on now suggests Kierkegaard's famous parable of the end of civilization. The setting is a theater. The leading actor in the play steps to the footlights and, in calm tones (lest he terrify the audience with the news and start a panic) tells them that the theater is on fire backstage. The audience, thinking the entire thing a hoax, a vaudeville act, applauds loudly. The actor, in anguish, renews his plea that they leave quietly and quickly. But each time, the audience applauds louder than before. This continues until all are trapped and perish in the flames.

We cannot say we have not been told what to expect if we continue our unregenerate ways of dealing with one another. We have been told a hundred different ways; it has been written in letters so large that he who runs may read. But it is not yet clear that we are preparing to heed the warning that all will soon be lost—irrevocably lost—if we do not build new spiritual foundations for our life and day.

II

Our spiritual plight did not spring upon us unawares. It had its prophets in the distant as well as the immediate past. Their warnings were hailed as the croakings of Cassandra; they themselves were dismissed as "queer."

Over a hundred years ago Henry Thoreau, one of the keenest

minds ever to be developed in this country, correctly diagnosed the nature of the trend then plainly discernible in human affairs: "We have improved means for reaching unimproved ends." But that sort of judgment did not make sense to a people busy conquering a continent, to an age in the early throes of the industrial revolution, or to anyone still intoxicated with the heady wines of the French and American revolutions. So they set Thoreau's judgment lightly to one side, asking what else could you expect from a crank who would forsake the cosmopolitanism of Boston for the solitude of Walden Pond. They then settled down to perfect the new means (which Thoreau did not criticize) for reaching the old ends (which he most assuredly did criticize).

Though Thoreau's contemporaries could laugh at him we cannot. We have seen his prediction verified. Mr. Raymond Fosdick, writing early in 1946, gives this description of the modern world: "Our technologies have far outrun both our moral sense and our social organization. Our wisdom about ends does not match our skill about means, and a great gulf has opened between our engineering and our ethics, between our knowledge and our ways of life. . . . The enemies that threaten us are our own creation: they are the techniques we have perfected and which we have allowed to be perverted to unworthy ends." [5]

Nor have our latter-day prophets been unworthy of the mantle of Thoreau. Oswald Spengler wrote his *Decline of the West* in 1914. While there is much unnecessary intellectual machinery in his notion of the cyclic theory of history, there can be no doubt that his book correctly interpreted the titanic forces of destruction which were rushing Europe and the West into a series of utterly ruinous wars. Although he was presented to my college generation as the laughable prophet of unrelieved pessimism, he stands before us now as something of an optimist because he, knowing nothing of the rapid strides in technology that were in the offing of his day, thought our civilization might last for a hundred years or more before succumbing to the internal forces of destruction.

Professor Arnold J. Toynbee, England's celebrated historian, is not much more optimistic than Spengler in his tremendous *Study of History*. He spends the first three volumes studying the genesis and growth of civilizations and the last three, their breakdowns and disintegrations. It is an altogether disquieting piece of work. Of the twenty-six civilizations that we are able to enumerate, "no less than sixteen . . . are by now dead and buried." After due consideration, Dr. Toynbee dismisses the idea that "these break-downs of civilization are . . . brought about by the operation, either recurrent or progressive, of cosmic forces which are out-side human control. . . ." [6] He then lists the reasons for the dis-appearance of the sixteen dead civilizations, and, presumably, all deal with factors clearly *within human control*. Some of them have an alarmingly contemporary ring: (1) the intractability of institutions; (2) the idolization of an ephemeral self; (3) the idolization of an ephemeral institution; (4) the idolization of an ephemeral technique; (5) the suicidalness of militarism; (6) the intoxication of victory. If history means anything at all, we must either neutralize at once and eventually eliminate these factors from modern life, or perish through their victory. This fateful alternative is clearly seen and singled out in one of the finest documents produced by Christian churchmen during recent years, a study of "The Relation of the Church to the War in the Light of the Christian Faith." When the psychologist says that our spiritual wells are empty; when the philosopher says that we have the wrong standards of value; when the historian says we are worshipping the wrong kind of gods; when a discerning student of literature says we are lost in the material and moral jungles of the world—the churchmen say, in effect, "Our sins have found us out. We are in the hands of the 'living God,' to whom we must answer for our ways."

No one has caught the keenness of the urgency of our situation better than Stephen Vincent Benét in his poem, "Song for Three Soldiers": * The poet visualizes three soldiers approaching out of the gloom, and he hails each in turn with a question that the soldier answers:

* Copyright, 1943, by Rosemary Benét.

Oh, where are you coming from, soldier, fine soldier,
In your dandy new uniform, all spick-and-span,
With your helmeted head and the gun on your shoulder,
Where are you coming from, gallant young man?

    I come from the war that was yesterday's trouble,
    I come with the bullet still blunt in my breast;
    Though long was the battle and bitter the struggle,
    Yet I fought with the bravest, I fought with the best.

Oh, where are you coming from, soldier, tall soldier,
With ray-gun and sun-bomb and everything new,
And a face that might well have been carved from a boulder,
Where are you coming from, now tell me true!

    My harness is novel, my uniform other
    Than any gay uniform people have seen,
    Yet I am your future and I am your brother
    And I am the battle that has not yet been.

Oh, where are you coming from, soldier, gaunt soldier,
With weapons beyond any reach of my mind,
With weapons so deadly the world must grow older
And die in its tracks, if it does not turn kind?

    Stand out of my way and be silent before me!
    For none shall come after me, foeman or friend,
    Since the seed of your seed called me out to employ me,
    And that was the longest and that was the end.[7]

III

One thing is sure: though we may have muddled our way into the spiritual plight just described, we are not going to be able to muddle our way out. If we get out (and that is a big *if*), it will be because we discard as wholly unreliable the kind of spiritual and moral maps we have been using and, for the most part, continue to use.

One of Britain's statesmen, Lord Salisbury, in the days of her imperial expansion, was fond of saying to his colleagues in Parliament, "You need to study larger maps!" Whether that was what was wrong with the maps they were using is open to serious question, but something was wrong. Be that as it may, his diagnosis of their trouble lays bare one of the great deficiencies of the modern world—something has been and is wrong with the maps by which we are trying to find our way.

Some of our maps are too small. They are drawn in terms of "I, me, and mine" instead of "we, us, and ours." They reflect the famous view of the editorial writer of a London paper who wanted to tell his readers of a severe channel storm; he headlined it with this amazing phrase, "Continent Isolated"! They reflect the views of some of our school children in Frederick County, Maryland. Their teacher was trying to get them interested in some of the faraway places of the world, but they were obviously unmoved. Taking advantage of our far-flung battle line, she said to one boy, "You ought to be interested in India. Your brother is there right now." "Yes," replied the boy, "but he wants to get back to Frederick County!"

There is something so essentially human and unquestionably good about that sort of attitude that you hate to lay critical hands upon it. Yet one of the most persistent ironies of life is the way in which something which begins as a great good can, if developed uncritically, become a great evil. Self-awareness, for example, is essential to the wholesome growth of the human personality. So also is self-interest. They are creative necessities in the development of our personality from infancy to maturity. They must, therefore, be accounted good. But when we reach the level of self-interest we find ourselves facing one of the deepest and most difficult decisions of life. The road of the developing personality forks at that point. We can proceed in one of two directions: self-centeredness or social-centeredness. Self-centeredness is evil not because it places a high valuation on the self but because it tries to arrest the normal exfoliation of the self in terms of larger and larger relationships and responsibilities. Social-centeredness is good, not because it ignores the self, but because it understands the proper conditions for its further growth. Both self-centeredness and social-centeredness are attempts at self-realization, but they lead to two radically different conceptions of the ideal self. Self-centeredness received its perfect statement from a young man who was applying for the job as usher in a theater. When asked by the manager what he would do in case of fire, he answered, "Oh, don't worry about me! I'd get out all right!" Social-centeredness received its perfect statement from another young man who said, "Greater love hath no man than this, that he lay down his life for his friends."

The same tremendous truth is hammering its way into the contemporary world. Nation-awareness and nation-concern are good, but nation-centeredness is evil and must be forsaken for world-centeredness. No one nation is more or less guilty than another of this great crime of inflated nationalism. All have stood at the fork in the road and all have chosen to "get out all right" rather than to "lay down their lives" for others. Sovereignty or the right to be completely independent in action and policy is the political name we give to nation-centeredness. Nations can continue to choose the road which it indicates but, having chosen it, they cannot choose to avoid the deathtrap into which it leads, except by an open and thoroughly sincere reversal of attitude and policy alike. To say that the nations of the modern world have chosen that road is to repeat a truism. To express the hope that they will reverse themselves before it is too late is to state the crucial question before the modern world.

Just as some of our maps are too small, others are plainly distorted by certain predilections of the map maker. The geopoliticians of Europe and America—men like Karl Haushofer and N. J. Spykman—have given us a fascinating set of maps. The basic principle in their construction is that material power guarantees security. Consequently they center attention upon certain "heart-lands" of power computed in terms of mineral resources and manpower. They advise us that whoever would survive the grim struggle for existence must possess or be allied with some such heart-land and let his entire life be controlled by that relationship. As information about the power potential of various areas of the world, such maps have their place. But when they begin to draw their moral for individual and national life, they are more than suspect, they are condemned out of hand. They blandly assume that the only thing essential to survival is the possession of the kind of power you can dig out of the bowels of the earth. They know nothing of justice, or right, or freedom. They counsel us to "keep power and purpose together" with power always being the determiner of decision.

Probably all we need to say about such maps is that as explanations of how we got where we are they are unexcelled. But as guides to the future, they are no more reliable than John Smith's first map of the Atlantic seaboard of America would be to the captain of the *Queen Mary*. I once showed the captain of a much smaller ship a facsimile of Smith's map and asked him if he would attempt to approach the coast guided only by it. He studied it for a moment and then replied, "Naw! I'd just jump overboard out here and drown comfortable-like!"

We in churches have scant reason for pointing the finger of shame at nations because of the kind of maps they have been using. We have been guilty of the same sin. Some of our maps plainly display creedal bias or sectarian bitterness or denominational rivalry. All such belong to an embittered and ineffectual yesterday rather than to a promising tomorrow. One of the most discouraging things about contemporary discussions of church union is the way in which the plan, presented at any given time, reflects the ecclesiastical background of the one who presents it. We have not yet learned to treasure our likenesses more than our differences in interdenominational thinking and living. What is needed more than anything else just now is the ability to draw the ecumenical outline over the sectarian outline in Christian thought and life. There is nothing which separates us half as important as that which unites us. We are not separated by a single theological doctrine or a single denominational position that comes even close to being as important as the many things that unite us. If we had an unlimited amount of time at our disposal to work out the *modus vivendi* of co-operation, we could say that in another four or five hundred years we might be able to get it done. But we do not have that kind of time. Let us face frankly the fact that one of the most dangerous sins of the contemporary church has been and is the toleration of the fruits of sectarianism long after the reasons for sectarianism have been accepted as bankrupt by every thoughtful person.

The net result of using the wrong kind of maps in a world like this is precisely the kind of world we are living in just now. It is a world that practices human sacrifice on a scale undreamed of by the wildest savages known to history. It is a world that is fearful, hateful, and utterly dangerous to everyone and everything living in it. It is a world that is so callous to injustices that only the keenest kind of event can touch it to the quick of its conscience any more. It takes the wholesale destruction of a city like Hiroshima to awaken us to the horror of killing noncombatants without any sense of discrimination. It takes the realization that six million Jews have been killed in Europe to awaken us to the unmitigated evil of racial and religious intolerance here or anywhere else. It takes the portrait of a Polish mother weeping over the body of her three-year-old boy, just dead of starvation, to make us realize that we are confronted with the absolute necessity of sharing the food we have with those who need it worse, and doing it at once.

IV

The late Archbishop Temple once made the penetrating observation: "The Church which comes out of this war without being radically changed will not be worthy of the name of Church." How can it be otherwise? What sort of people would we be if times like these did not burn their mark into our very soul? The church must be willing to be remade even as it seeks to remake the world in fidelity to its ancient task. What is it, in a sentence, that we propose to do?

We propose to get a Christ-sized map of mankind and to be guided by that rather than by any other, lesser map. This is the map which we propose to use in our evaluation of the principles and policies of peoples, churches, and nations alike. Our motive in using it will be the ancient and honorable Christian motive of love of God and love of man. The method in using it will be that of persuasion rather than coercion, sharing rather than dominating, serving rather than being served. To use this kind of map rather than any lesser kind is no mere difference of words. It means, concretely, a movement away from disunity toward unity, from discord to community, from a sense of being lost to an awareness of communion in God's will for us and for all mankind.

This sort of evangelization must begin at home, with the church and the immediate community. Once at work there, its application can and will embrace larger and larger groups. The indigenous church in each country must assume the responsibility of the spiritual welfare of the people among whom its lot is cast. We happen to be living in America—a nation in which every major problem known to mankind is up for consideration and decision. Some of these problems have to do with our foreign policy, some with the direction we take in industrial relations, and some with racial relations.

For example, the burning question before the American people just now is: What shall be our policy in international relations? Are we going to lapse back into isolationism? Or are we going to move ahead into a kind of imperialism? Or are we, as a third alternative, going to lead the way into a new and genuine kind of co-operation among the nations of the world? This is an explosive alternative just now. The ghost of isolationism seems to be pretty effectively laid by contemporary events, but not so the specter of imperialism. That is a great danger before America today. It is interesting to study the various ways in which we seek to justify it, even cover it up. For example, we are laying claims to many islands in the Pacific for "security reasons," says the Navy Department. But if we do secure a mandate for the islands now claimed by the Navy, we become the dominating power in the Pacific. Thus we accentuate an imperialistic impulse which has never been absent from American history since the Spanish-American War. Only this time it will be imperialism on a world-wide scale, and for keeps. Small wonder Russia, China,

Australia, and Japan are concerned about our aspirations in the Pacific. It is an ominous thing that a ranking Australian general has been quoted to the effect that, incredible as it seems, Australia must consider the possibility of war with the United States! He says that the Manus Island lease desired by the Navy Department of the United States constitutes a direct threat to the security of Australia. Evidently there is some ambiguity in our intentions as they unfold in economic, political, and military policies!

The only alternative which really interests the Christian thinker on international policy is *genuine co-operation*—a co-operation not based primarily on the Big Three, the Big Five, or the Security Council but upon the realization that the community of nations is the real custodian both of moral values and of the common security of all. Power becomes the servant of virtue only when power is subordinated to law and justice. Unless it is so controlled, it will do little but secure privilege and is certain to be misused. Fortunately, in the United Nations we see the beginnings of the attempt to share the responsibility of power. We have a long way to go yet, but we can be grateful for the fact that even a beginning has been made in times like these. We can continue to work and pray for the day when that beginning will become a full-fledged development. One of the proudest chapters of the history of the church is the way in which it helped awaken the people of this country to the importance of beginning but not being content with the United Nations as it is.

We are all doing a lot of thinking about the tension which is erupting in a mild form of civil war in the industrial structure of America. What direction are we as a nation going to take as we seek a solution to this problem?

In another connection we noted Dr. Arnold Toynbee's opinion that the basic conflict in the modern world is between modern industrialism on the one hand and democracy on the other.[8] Democracy is the conqueror of the political theory of the divine right of kings. Democracy says that each man is a bearer of infinite worth because he is a child of God. Democracy says, further, that man is entitled to have a voice in the determination of the laws under which he lives and the government which administers the laws. It took nearly two hundred years of hard fighting for democracy to overthrow one type of tyranny after another in the political life of Europe a century or two ago. Now the spirit of democracy finds itself face to face with feudalism entrenched in industry. Modern industrialism is essentially feudal in structure, conferring upon a man or a small group of men the right to control the conditions under which a large number of people earn their livelihood.

Some of our contemporaries believe or pretend to believe that democracy can be confined to the political sphere and kept entirely out of the economic sphere. But they have yet to tell us how this can be done. Can you tell a man that he is a bearer of infinite work in the personal and political spheres without having it reverberate in the economic sphere? If this fact entitles him to a voice in the determination of laws and government, why does it not also entitle him to a voice in the determination of the policies and the principles of the industry in which he works? The alternative, plainly, is either less democracy in politics or more democracy in industry.

The church has no real choice in this matter. We must move in the direction of greater democracy in industry. There seems to be no other way to avert an increasing amount of confusion in the years that lie ahead. There is no other way to correct many existing evils in our industrial order. No one has a detailed blueprint as to how this should proceed, but if the large majority of us are willing to grant it as a necessary and legitimate end, the blueprint will be found. Just now what is most needed is the will to make the blueprint.

And, finally, what are we going to do about the color line, which has the whole world writhing in its coils? Living as we do in one world—a world of many races and colors—we who are white need to remember that the white race is the minority problem in the life of mankind. The great colored majority of mankind are on the march toward an equalization of rights and opportunities. One of Nehru's first acts upon assuming leadership in India was to call a conference of the "subjugated peoples" of Asia! We in the white race have the power just now but, over the period of a hundred or more years, there is little reason to doubt that they will be the possessors of enough power to curb if not overthrow stubborn minorities like us. I do not suppose it is possible to make a fresh attempt at the color problem (history seems to have no reverse-gear), but I am convinced that we, in churches, must be willing to give up a stubborn persistence in the wrong answers of segregation and discrimination. The only proper place to begin is in church life and polity. Here again detailed blueprints are lacking, but what is more tragically true is that the will to find the blueprints is, itself, lacking. It is precisely at the point of a reluctant will-to-do-good that the Christian faith can make a beginning in a person or a people. As we will to solve the color problem, we shall be able to find the blueprint for the proper and equitable solution. That is the peril and the promise of all interfaith and interracial movements within the Christian churches at the present time. A new answer must be found and it can be found only by those *who seek "with all their heart."*

V

These are some of our problems as we try to evangelize America. We must dedicate ourselves to the task of measuring our country and our churches against the Christ-sized map which gives us our sense of direction. Needless to say, we will beware of short, pat answers. But we must be in the forefront of those who are willing to find the right answer—God's answer—the only one that is *an answer*. We must define our destiny as a nation in terms of world order and as a church in terms of a world community.

But, you ask, isn't that risky? Of course, but not half as risky as trying to stay where we are just now. People who complain about the risk involved in moving in new directions these days remind me of a boyhood friend who barely escaped a fatal accident as a result of wanting to stay put when he needed to move. A street in the small town where he lived was being widened, and the workmen were blasting stumps away from the edge of the pavement. On this particular morning they had placed a huge charge of dynamite under one stump and lighted a providentially long fuse to it. We had no sooner taken cover, awaiting the explosion, when the boy to whom I refer ran out of a near-by house, perched himself squarely on the stump that was about to go up and began munching an apple! Of course he know nothing of what was happening and, to make matters worse, his mother came out of the house just then. When she heard the workmen shouting at her boy, she called to him, "Phillip, stay right where you are! If they hurt you, they'll pay for it!" Fortunately one of the workmen was able to get him off the stump and down to the ground in time to avoid being hurt by the blast. Unfortunately, there are many people who seem to want us to sit right where we are even though we know full well that a huge charge of dynamite has been placed under the *status quo* of the world. It is risky business moving, but not half as risky as staying where we are.

No one will underestimate the gravity of the undertaking which we are considering. An aroused, aggressive, reborn Christian church has neither need nor place for the fainthearted in its pews. And if there is one place where such should not be, it is the Christian pulpit. That, assuredly, is no place for middle-of-the-roaders, for men who want to carry water on both shoulders. If the Christian church seeks a detour around the realistic problems we have been considering, it will be preaching Christ as a form of words, not as a way of life. This is no time for the Church to seek "safe men" for positions of responsible leadership. They must be willing to risk, to brave, to dare, and to do with a courage unexcelled in Christian history.

Ours is one of the greatest opportunities and proudest obligations in the two thousand years of Christian history—*to make the Christian gospel a real alternative in the thinking and the living of men.* To do this will be to move in new directions. It will mean making many mistakes. But we must take that chance. As I understand it, the specific purpose of the gospel is to turn the world inside out and upside down. We are trying to create first of ourselves and then of other people "new creatures in Christ." When Christ enters into a man, he is a new person, and when Christ enters into a social order, it will be a new social order. That is our historic task.

Notes

Chapter I: CONFRONTING THE SPIRITUAL TRAGEDY OF OUR TIME

[1] Quoted in the New York *Times*, December 10, 1939.

[2] Edna St. Vincent Millay, *Conversation at Midnight* (New York: Harper & Brothers, 1937), p. 29.

[3] Quotations from "French and American Pessimism," *Harper's Magazine*, September, 1945.

[4] Arnold Toynbee, *Study of History* (New York: Oxford University Press, 1939), VI, 178 ff.

Chapter II: SKEPTICISM KNOWS NO ANSWER

[1] Bagobert B. Runes (ed.), *Dictionary of Philosophy* (New York: The Philosophical Library, 1942), pp. 277-278. While leaning heavily on the article "Scepticism," I have combined some meanings and reworded others. This publication as well as the Encyclopaedia Britannica uses the English spelling of the word.

[2] "How Shall We Think of God?" in Thomas S. Kepler (ed.), *Contemporary Religious Thought* (Nashville: Abingdon-Cokesbury Press, 1941).

[3] Herman Rauschning, *The Revolution of Nihilism* (New York: Alliance Book Corporation, 1939), pp. 100 f.

[4] *Ibid.*, p. 104.

[5] Lectures at the Institute of International Relations, Greensboro, North Carolina, 1943.

[6] J. H. Randall, Jr., *Making of the Modern Mind* (Boston: Houghton Mifflin Co., 1926), p. 560.

[7] Bertrand Russell, *Sceptical Essays* (New York: W. W. Norton and Co., 1928).

[8] Bertrand Russell, *Mysticism and Logic* (New York: Longmans, Green and Co., 1918).

[9] Cf. Sir William Cecil Dampier, *History of Science* (New York: The Macmillan Company, 1942), chap. vii.

[10] Sir James Jeans, *Physics and Philosophy* (New York: The Macmillan Company, 1943), chap. iv.

[11] *Ibid.*, p. 42.

[12] *Ibid.*, p. 110.

[13] *Ibid.*, p. 216.

[14] Robert Browning, "Fra Lippo Lippi."

[15] Rackham Holt, *George Washington Carver* (New York: Doubleday, Doran and Co., 1943), p. 220.

[16] Quoted in *ibid.*, p. 268.

[17] I have developed this point in greater detail in *The Philosophical Heritage of the Christian Faith* (Chicago: Willett, Clark and Co., 1944), chap. ii.

[18] *Laws*, Book X.

[19] Will Durant, *Story of Philosophy* (Garden City: Garden City Publishing Co., 1926), p. 300.

[20] Lois Kingsley Pelton, "Iconoclast." The New York *Times*, July 17, 1943.

[21] N. Hartmann, *Ethics* (New York: The Macmillan Company, 1932), II, 294.

[22] *Life*, June 10, 1946.

Chapter III: CAN THE BLIND LEAD THE BLIND?

[1] Jacques Barzun, *Of Human Freedom* (Boston: Little, Brown and Co., 1939), p. 36.

[2] *General Education in a Free Society* (Cambridge: Harvard University Press, 1945), p. 4.

[3] Oxford Conference Books (Chicago: Willett, Clark and Co., 1938).

Chapter IV: IS A NEW PERSPECTIVE POSSIBLE?

[1] Samuel Nathaniel Behrman, *The Talley Method*, when presented in Baltimore.

[2] Walter van Kirk, *A Christian Global Strategy* (Chicago: Willett, Clark and Co., 1945), p. 116.

[3] Leo Tolstoy, *My Religion*, p. 237.

[4] Oxford Conference Books (Chicago: Willett, Clark and Co., 1938).

[5] Ephesians 4:12.

[6] Arthur Holt, *This Nation Under God* (Chicago: Willett, Clark and Co., 1939), p. 151.

[7] Quoted in Homrighausen, *Let the Church Be the Church* (Nashville: Abingdon-Cokesbury Press, 1940), p. 65.

[8] *This Nation Under God*, p. 179. Another book, *Christian Routes of Democracy in America* (New York: Friendship Press, 1941), adds a store of rich information to the position advanced in *This Nation Under God*.

[9] M. Searles Bates, *Religious Liberty, an Inquiry* (New York: International Missionary Council, 1945).

[10] Paul Hutchinson, *The New Leviathan* (Chicago: Willett, Clark and Co., 1945).

[11] *Op. cit.*, p. 582.

[12] *Op. cit., passim*, pp. 226 ff.
[13] Paul Efrick Eldridge, in *Opinion*, 1946.

Chapter V: RELIGIOUS LIBERALISM POINTS THE WAY

[1] Quoted in Catherine Drinker Bowen, *Yankee from Olympus* (Boston: Little, Brown and Co., 1944), p. 197.

[2] Reinhold Niebuhr, *The Nature and Destiny of Man* (New York: Charles Scribner's Sons, 1941), II, 185.

[3] *Ibid.*, II, 199.

[4] David E. Roberts and Henry Pitney van Dusen (eds.), *Liberal Theology* (New York: Charles Scribner's Sons, 1942), p. 108.

[5] Referred to in chap. i, p. 9.

Chapter VI: THE CHURCH CHAMPIONS THE COMMON MAN

[1] Much of the material in this chapter was worked out in the deliberations of a seminar which assisted in the preparation for the Conference on the Christian Basis of World Order, called by the Methodist Church at Delaware, Ohio, in 1943. I am deeply indebted to the twenty men, laymen as well as ministers, who constituted the seminar and whose judgments found their way into the report which was presented to the conference. Although I had the privilege of writing and presenting the report at that time and have rewritten it for this book, much of it is the product of one of the most interesting efforts in group thinking I have experienced.

[2] E. H. Carr, *Conditions of Peace* (New York: The Macmillan Company, 1942).

[3] *The Spectator*, December 4, 1942, p. 519; not all English reaction was so favorably inclined toward the report.

[4] Herbert Agar, *A Time for Greatness* (Boston: Little, Brown and Co., 1942), p. 26.

[5] H. P. Jordan (ed.), *Problems of Post-War Reconstruction* (Washington: American Council on Public Affairs, 1942), pp. 42 ff.

[6] Cf. Leland Stowe, "Hungary's Agrarian Revolution," *Foreign Affairs*, April, 1947, pp. 490 ff.

[7] Cf. L. H. Bailey, *The Holy Earth* (New York: Christian Rural Fellowship, 1943), and other background books.

[8] Arnold Toynbee, *Study of History* (New York: Oxford University Press, 1939), I, *passim*.

[9] Report of Delaware Conference, 1942.

[10] Social Creed of the Methodist Church.

[11] *Information Service*, January 11, 1947. Published by the Federal Council of Churches of Christ in America.

[12] Ernest Troeltoch, *The Social Teaching of the Christian Churches* (New York: The Macmillan Company, 1931), I, 23.

Chapter VII: RELIGIOUS FAITH UNDERGIRDS DEMOC-
RACY

1 Will Durant, *The Life of Greece* (New York: Simon & Schuster, Inc.,
1939), chap. xviii, pp. 437 ff.

2 *Ibid.*, p. 554.

3 T. V. Smith, "Contemporary Perplexities in Democratic Theory," *International Journal of Ethics,* XXXI, 14.

4 In *The Prince.*

5 In *The Leviathan.*

6 "Locksley Hall."

7 Madras Series, I-VII, International Missions Council, *passim.*

8 Malvern Conference Report.

9 *A Message to the Churches.* The Commission on a Just and Durable
Peace, 297 Fourth Avenue, New York, New York, p. 8.

10 F. R. Barry, *What Has Christianity to Say?* (New York: Harper &
Brothers, 1938), p. 31.

Chapter VIII: A NEW CHURCH WORKS FOR A NEW
WORLD

1 Testimony before the House Military Affairs Committee, February 18,
1946.

2 As reported in the New York *Times,* June 16, 1946.

3 Paul Hutchinson, "Christian Missions and Imperialism," in *Christian
World Mission* (Nashville: Commission on Ministerial Training, the Methodist Church, 1946).

4 *A Message to the Churches.* From the National Study Conference,
Cleveland, Ohio, January 15-19, 1945.

5 Memorandum, Cleveland Conference, published by the Federal Council
of Churches.

6 Quoted in *Christendom,* XI, 211.

7 Theodore Wedel, *The Coming Great Church* (New York: The Macmillan Company, 1945).

8 *Christendom* is the magazine "voice" of the World Council in the
United States. Each issue carries news of the growth of the ecumenical
spirit and movement.

9 *Op. cit.,* p. 24.

10 H. A. Wallace and others, *The Christian Basis of World Order* (Nashville: Abingdon-Cokesbury Press, 1943). The Merric Lectures.

11 Walter van Kirk, *A Christian Global Strategy* (Chicago: Willett, Clark
and Co., 1945).

12 W. K. Anderson (ed.), *Christian World Mission* (Nashville: Commission on Ministerial Training, the Methodist Church, 1946).

13 Cf. Truman Douglass' brilliant article, "Directing Our Holy Impatience
for Christian Unity," *Christendom,* XII, 93 ff.

[14] E. Stanley Jones, "The Price of Ultimate Victory," in *Christian World Mission*.

[15] *A Christian Global Strategy*, p. 188.

[16] Josiah Royce, *Spirit of Modern Philosophy* (Boston: Houghton Mifflin Co., 1892), p. 216.

Chapter IX: "WHILE TIME REMAINS"

[1] Kenneth Scott Latourette, *A History of the Expansion of Christianity*, I-VII (New York: Harper & Brothers), 1938-45, *passim*.

[2] E. B. Krumbhow (professor of history, University of Pennsylvania), "The Concept of Internationalism," *Science*, January 26, 1945.

[3] Paul Hutchinson, *The New Leviathan* (Chicago: Willett, Clark and Co., 1946).

[4] *Ibid.*, p. 180.

[5] New York *Times* Magazine, January, 1946.

[6] *Study of History*, IV, 39.

[7] Stephen Vincent Benet, "Song for Three Soldiers."

[8] *Study of History*, I, chap. vi.

INDEX